Lynn Gordon

Published in 2018 by Penley Publishing

Copyright © Lynn Gordon 2018

Lynn Gordon has asserted her right to be identified as the author of this Work in accordance with the Copyright, Designs and Patents Act 1988

ISBN Paperback: 978-1-9995823-0-2
Ebook: 978-1-9995823-1-9

All rights reserved. No part of this publication may be reproduced, stored in a retrieval system, or transmitted in any form or by any means, electronic, mechanical, photocopying, recording or otherwise, without the prior permission of the copyright owner.

A CIP catalogue copy of this book can be found in the British Library.

Published with the help of Indie Authors World
www.indieauthorsworld.com

DEDICATION

FOR ALICE AND DEREK, ALWAYS IN MY THOUGHTS –. FOREVER IN MY HEART

ACKNOWLEDGEMENTS

There are so many people, without whom, this book may never have been achievable.

To those members of my family, (you know who you are), whose unwavering support and comfort during some of the darkest moments detailed in my story, I give my sincere thanks and love.

To my niece Mandy, thank you for all your hard work in helping to design and illustrate the front cover, grateful thanks also go to Justine for your input.

To Janet and Carl for your support and comfort during the difficult period outlined in Iris's story.

To the wonderful girls from the care Company formerly known as Crossroads, your contribution to Mum's care was immense and I send my heartfelt thanks to each of you.

To Visibility, Glasgow, a charitable organisation providing help and support to people living with sight loss. Thank you for helping me find my way around the technology which has allowed me to write my book. Special thanks to Graham and his guide dog Toffee, who taught me the basics which allowed me to get started.

To Guide Dogs association, thanks for your information re 'guide dogs and mental health'

To the Royal National Institution for the Blind, (RNIB) for being there!

To Allison, my Editor, thank you so much for all your help and guidance.

To my friend John, thanks for reading my drafts and providing invaluable feedback, very much appreciated.

Finally, to Kim and Sinclair of Indie Authors World without whom this book would simply not have been possible.

PART ONE

1

SO CONFUSED

"Is there anybody here, can somebody help me?"

The voice seems to come from afar and I'm not sure whether I am dreaming. In an instant I am out of bed and on my feet, scrambling to my mum's aide – she is outside my room and perilously close to the top of the stairs.

I berate myself for having drifted off and not hearing her get out of bed as I take Mum's hand and tell her gently, "It's OK Mum, I'm here, it is the middle of the night; do you want to go back to bed?"

Mum hesitates as if digesting my words and says, "I need to pee." I ease her into the bathroom and turn her so she is standing in front of the toilet. She remains perfectly still for several seconds and appears not to know what to do.

"Are you OK Mum?"

"Where am I?" she asks.

I remind her that she wanted to use the toilet and gently help her to get sorted, then guide her back into bed. I wait outside her room until satisfied that she has drifted off to sleep and then return to my own bed where I lie awake listening for movement from Mum's room.

My bedside clock tells me it is 3:26am and this is the third time tonight Mum has wandered out of her room in a confused state.

I have been staying with Mum for the past week; she is becoming increasingly confused and my two sisters and I are spending more and more time with her.

This has been our family home for over forty years, having moved to the 'new town' in August 1965 from the two up two down 'Coronation Street' style house in the heart of Liverpool.

I remember with such clarity, the day Mum and Dad (Annie and Dennis) brought us to Brookvale to view the house. I was eight years old; it was the middle of the school summer holidays.

My two sisters, Eleanor; age ten and Jane, just five and me ran through the spacious house squealing with delight.

"Three bedrooms, three bedrooms, yipee; I get my own room at last," Eleanor cannot contain her excitement.

There is a fairly large garden at the back and a smaller one which has a tree slap bang in the middle to the front of the terraced house which is soon to become our new home.

Two gardens and a tree! I am thrilled. The closest we had been to any greenery was when we were taken for a special day out to one of the urban parks around Liverpool.

Brookvale was a relatively new town built in the Fifties to accommodate families from the old Victorian homes in Liverpool, many of which had been destroyed or damaged during the war.

Our new home was situated in a quiet crescent with a selection of semi-detached, terraced and three story flats, all had gardens to the front, but our new home was one of a very few which had a tree.

Two of Mum's sisters and their families lived in another part of the town. They lived in flats which we had visited many times during our early childhood; but we were to live in a 'proper house', with not just one, but two gardens and a tree of our own. It really was something pretty special.

Mum now lives here alone since Dad passed away two years ago following a short illness. My two sisters live close by – Jane and her family are only a short walk away and Eleanor lives in a nearby town around five miles from Mum.

I am two hundred miles away having moved to Scotland in the summer of 1982.

2

FOREVER CHANGED

TWO YEARS EARLIER – 8 NOVEMBER 2005

"Hurry up you two, you'll be late if you don't get a move on."

It's Mum; she is standing at the foot of the stairs and shouting up to Dad and I as I finish dressing. My dad is in the bathroom showering and getting ready for the hospital appointment where he is to undergo a colonoscopy.

Eleanor, now fifty, sporting a suntan from her recent trip to the Bahamas where she and Jack had celebrated their thirtieth wedding anniversary, arrived a little while ago and is in the kitchen finishing a cup of tea with Mum.

Eleanor, like myself and Jane, is partially blind. We have all inherited the degenerative eye condition, Retinitis Pigmentosa (RP) which has long since rendered Mum and three of her siblings totally blind.

"Are you sure you don't want to come with us?" Eleanor asks.

"No," Mum responds. "There are plenty of you going; Dad can tell me all about it when he gets home," adding, "I shouldn't think you will be too long."

We are just awaiting the arrival of my niece Julie, Eleanor's eldest daughter, and Jane; then we will be off. Talk about mob-handed, but that's the way it has always been in my family; if ever anyone has a problem or ailment, we are all there offering support and just generally being around for each other.

My dad, God bless him, having lived in a houseful of females, is the most patient, placid person I have ever known, with a gentle nature and unconscious wit which never ceases to bring a giggle to me and my sisters and prompt Mum to proclaim with a wry smile 'soft old git." This is one of her many terms of endearment when referring to Dad.

I remember Mum and Dad coming home from a holiday in Blackpool where they had taken a sightseeing trip in a helicopter along the coastline. Because Mum is blind, Dad thought it would be amusing to request a discount for Mum who wouldn't be doing much seeing. This tickled us when he relayed the story but prompted Mum to mutter this term of endearment in her amusement.

Normally when we all gather at Mum and Dad's house in the morning, Mum will be pottering around with some bits of housework, or else listening to an audio book, whilst Dad, who retired several years earlier from his job in a local light engineering firm, will be reading his morning paper. Then he will cook sausages and we all sit around the kitchen table where we spend many happy hours enjoying sausage butties and a cup of tea, just chatting and laughing and generally putting the world to rights.

This morning however we aren't considering stuffing ourselves with goodies as poor old Dad has been on a starvation diet for twenty-four hours, as well as undergoing a 'clearing out' process in preparation for the procedure he is about to undergo. Little do any of us realise that our lives will be changed forever in just a few hours' time.

Eleanor and I sit either side of Dad in an anteroom following the procedure, after being told someone will be along shortly to discuss the test results. We then stare speechless and with disbelief at the nurse who delivers the news that they have found a cancer in my dad's bowel. I take hold of Dad's hand and squeeze it; he is nodding his head at the nurse but by this time I'm not able to take in much of what she is saying. When I look back at this moment, I realise that Dad was incredibly calm and accepting of what he was being told; it was as though the nurse was merely confirming something he already knew. Everything was a haze and I just about heard a strangled sob escape from someone. I don't know which of us was responsible.

I hear the nurse tell us she will leave us for a few minutes and Eleanor goes outside to tell the others the awful news. By this time, Molly, Jane's eldest daughter, has arrived and is in the waiting room with Jane and Julie. The nurse comes back and confirms she has arranged another test for later that afternoon, explaining it is the next step in ascertaining the extent of the cancer and it will be beneficial to have it done today so that Dad will not have to go through the 'clearing out' process again.

We gather ourselves and head to another area of the hospital where the next test, a barium enema, will be carried out.

Eleanor phones Mum to say that we will be a bit longer than we thought; she doesn't tell her any more.

We arrive back at Mum and Dad's house where we are met by Mum who is in a foul mood, or so it seems. We can't possibly have known this was just a tiny glimpse of what lay ahead.

We are hardly in the door when Mum shouts at no-one in particular, "I wanted to go with you, why did you go without me?" The furious nature of her next words go through me like a knife. None of us, including Dad, have said much at this point, instead Dad attempts to sooth Mum, asking her to sit down then telling Eleanor to make everyone some tea. Mum hardly gives Dad a chance to finish speaking when she begins shouting at us, "fuck off, get out of my house; fuck off the lot of you."

I am stupefied at this outburst; Mum has never used such language before. My dad never swore either, at least not in our presence although he was a Royal Marine Commando for nine years in his younger days, seeing plenty of action in hostile places. He spent eighteen months in Cyprus during hostilities between the Greek and Turkish Cypriots in the mid-fifties, as well as postings to Mogadishu and Algiers, so I'm sure he will have known and used some colourful language in his time, but he never once brought it into our home.

It is as though the mum we had left earlier that day has disappeared and someone else has taken over her body. She looks like our mum and moves like her but otherwise is unrecognisable. Again, Dad does not appear too phased at Mum's outburst but he surreptitiously gestures to me that we should leave him and Mum alone for a while.

We all go to our Auntie Iris who lives just two doors away and when she opens the door to us we are already tearful and probably incoherent.

Thank goodness for Iris; she is one of Mum's younger sisters; she too is blind and has lived alone since being widowed sixteen years ago. She and Uncle Henry lived within yards of our family home throughout our adolescence and growing up she was like a second mum to the three of us. Iris and Henry had no children and treated us as though we were their own.

As is typical of Iris, she remains calm and lets us babble on through our tears. We all sit around and, ever the pragmatist, Iris tries to assure us that a cancer diagnosis is not the end of the world.

"Not these days," she opines. "Look at Uncle John," she continues, her and Mum's only brother. "He lived with cancer for many years, there is so much that can be done nowadays, I'm sure your Dad will be OK."

I do not remember much else about that day but it will come to be a defining moment in our lives and will forever be known as the day our lives changed completely.

I remain at Mum and Dad's home for a few more days trying to digest the awful news before returning to my own home in Scotland. I have spoken to my husband Stewart every day and he is fully aware of the situation with Dad. Stewart is shocked and upset and tells me to stay with my family for as long as I need. As soon as I arrive home I just fall into his arms and weep as I have never done before.

Stewart tries to comfort me, offering the same reassurances as Iris had just days before, but there is no comfort to be had.

The thought of losing Dad is unbearable, he is only seventy-three and although he has suffered two heart attacks since February 1991, he enjoyed relatively good health until a few months ago when he started to tire easily and just did not seem to be himself. I put this down to his long-standing heart condition and generally getting older. Never for a moment did I imagine Dad would get cancer.

3

A VERY LONG DAY

It's Tuesday 13 December 2005. Mum and I have been up since around 6:00am. I guess neither of us slept too well. Eleanor has arrived and appears every bit as anxious as me.

We haven't said much about Dad's surgery which is scheduled for this morning. Mum seems reluctant to acknowledge our anxiety, becoming angry and bordering on aggressive when either of us mention Dad. We sit making small talk and after a while, Jane arrives.

"Is there any news?" she asks.

"Not yet," I say. "It's a bit too early for any word."

Jane seems really anxious, pacing up and down the lounge; she wants to phone the hospital. "Shall I phone?" she asks.

"If anybody is going to phone the hospital, it will be me," Mum exclaims in a tone which brooks no argument and so, for the umpteenth time this morning I say, "I'll put the kettle on shall I?"

Mum's tone softens as she asks whether there is anything to go with her cup of tea. I bring a box of doughnuts in from the kitchen which Eleanor brought with her and the four of us tuck in.

Eleanor was diagnosed with type 2 diabetes a few years ago and I am forever having a go at her for eating things she is not supposed to but I cannot bring myself to chastise her for the sugary treat at this stressful time.

An hour or so passes and Eleanor tries another approach. "Mum," she says as she returns from a visit to the bathroom, "when you were speaking to the nurse yesterday, did she say what time Dad would be back from theatre?" adding, "it's just that, if he doesn't get out until late in the day we may not be allowed to visit him tonight."

Mum surprises us as she stands up and heads for the phone saying, "Yes that's a thought, what is the number?"

I dial the number for her and she gets through to the ward. I stand as close to Mum as I dare in an attempt to hear the voice at the other end of the line.

Mum gives my dad's name and asks whether he has had his operation yet. Both Eleanor and I sigh in exasperation. It is only midday, too early to expect any news. Mum listens for a while. I cannot hear what is being said. Mum utters the occasional, "yes, OK," and after a beat, "OK, thanks," and with that the receiver is replaced.

The three of us sit in anticipation and when Mum returns to her chair without a word, I ask, "What did they say?" "What did who say?"

Mum answers, "Oh, I don't think he is having the operation today."

Eleanor's frustration is evident as she demands to know what the nurse had said. Mum ponders but no response comes our way.

"Why didn't you let me speak to them?" I ask. My own anxiety is barely contained. Mum is angry and Eleanor immediately goes over to her, sitting on the arm of the chair in which Mum is seated and puts her arm around Mum's shoulder.

"It's a worrying time for us isn't it Mum, but just think, this time next week we will be sitting around Dad's bed, he will be on the mend and might even be home before Christmas."

Mum seems calmer and asks, "Shall we have a cup of tea?"

I cannot face another cuppa but I go into the kitchen and make one for Mum.

Eleanor brings Mum into the kitchen and then goes upstairs where she phones the hospital and speaks to the ward sister, who explains that Dad's surgery has been postponed until Thursday because there was a serious accident in a local factory this morning so all the theatres are being utilised to treat casualties. I recall hearing something about it on the radio earlier.

I ask Mum whether she wants to go to afternoon visiting seeing as Dad will still be on the ward and we all agree to go to the hospital later.

Poor Dad, he is sitting up in bed and sounds fed up. He says he is starving which is not surprising as he has barely eaten since Sunday evening. He explains that he is going to theatre first thing Thursday morning so can have a light meal tonight and then nothing at all tomorrow. "I am wasting away to a warehouse," he says and we all give a little chuckle. This is one of Dad's funnies when anyone says they are on a diet. I never did quite get the connection but it tickled Dad and we always joined him in his mirth.

Mum and I attend afternoon visiting the following day whilst Eleanor, Jane and their families visit in the evening. Dad seems in good spirits. Eleanor tells me when she phoned the night before the operation she was told by the ward sister that Dad would definitely be going to theatre first thing in the morning. He would then be taken into the High Dependency Unit straight from theatre, where he would remain for a few days before being transferred into a surgical ward until his discharge. The ward sister explains that he will not be allowed any visitors tomorrow and instead we should phone in the afternoon to see how things have gone.

Talk about here we are again! Once more, Eleanor has arrived at Mum's house fairly early and Jane has said she will be here shortly.

"How was Mum last night?" Jane asks upon her arrival. I tell her Mum was in good fettle although she asked a couple of times why Dad hadn't had his operation yet. I had to explain about the accident and the theatres being unavailable and she seemed to understand but then asked me again a little while later whether Dad has still to have his operation.

I am exhausted having barely slept last night; the combination of worry over Dad, anxiety at Mum's increasing confusion, coupled with my sense of helplessness and uncertainty threaten to overwhelm me.

Eleanor tells me to go to bed for a couple of hours. She will be staying here for most of the day and will make sure Mum is alright. I take up her suggestion and fall into a fretful slumber.

I come back downstairs around midday as Eleanor is making sandwiches for lunch. We sit around the table but I have little appetite. Eleanor also seems to be playing around with her food. Jane has gone home for a little while as she has to collect her youngest daughter from nursery. I'm glad to see that Mum is tucking in with gusto and when she finishes her sandwiches she asks, "Is there anything else?" Eleanor produces an apple pie from the fridge and cuts Mum a slice.

"Do you want some cream on your pie?" she asks Mum.

"Ooh yes," Mum says. "That would be nice."

The three of us sit around the table while Mum finishes her pudding. No mention has been made of Dad since I came down after my sleep.

"Is there any word from the hospital?" I ask tentatively.

"Not so far." Eleanor responds.

Mum appears oblivious to my question; it is nearly 2:00pm and if things have gone according to plan, Dad should be out of theatre by now but neither of us want to mention anything for fear of upsetting Mum. Jane returns and we sit in meaningless conversation for a while with no news from the hospital and no indication from Mum that she wants to call them.

"Gosh," Jane exclaims, as her talking watch tells us it is 3:00pm. "Surely the operation will be over by now; shall we call and see how things are?"

She heads to the phone. Mum gets out of her chair and follows her, asking, "What's the number?" Jane dials for her. She seems to be accepting of this gesture but when Jane has finished dialing Mum immediately takes the phone from her and starts speaking before anyone has answered.

"I don't think you are through yet Mum," Jane tells her.

Then Jane hears the disembodied voice say, "Aintree University Hospital, which ward please?" Mum starts to explain that her husband was due to have an operation this morning.

"Can you tell me how he is please?"

At this point she has not been put through to anyone so is still on to the switchboard, nor has she given my dad's name so the person on the other end is understandably at a loss. Jane cannot hear what is being said on the other end of the phone but Mum responds, "I don't know, he has got cancer."

We are all becoming increasingly concerned as it is apparent that Mum is very confused and seems incapable of articulating her inquiry.

"Do you want me to speak to them?" Eleanor asks Mum.

She mumbles something and puts the phone down. We are none the wiser. Jane says she needs the bathroom and I am sure she intends phoning the hospital back from Mum's bedroom. There is so much tension in the room; Mum, Eleanor and I are sitting in the lounge and I put the radio on in an attempt to mask the sound of Jane moving around upstairs.

"What is she doing up there?" Mum proclaims as she goes to the door and shouts to Jane that she should come down at once. It is unbelievable how much fear she instills at this moment. Jane comes down right away and we all sit in silence, fearful of saying the wrong thing. My head starts to ache and the all too familiar sense of dread overwhelms me.

We remain like this for several minutes until Eleanor tells us she is going home for a while and we should let her know as soon as we hear Dad is out of theatre. Jane too goes home shortly afterwards; Mum and I listen to the radio and I tentatively suggest that we try the hospital again. Mum agrees but insists that she will speak to them. I dial the number and ask for the High Dependency Unit before handing the phone to Mum. She gives my dad's name, address and date of birth and asks how he is. Once again I hear Mum's responses, "hmmm, oh" and "OK thank you," before replacing the receiver.

I ask what they said. Like before, Mum is vague and I am no wiser. I try another tack.

"Is he out of theatre yet?"

"I don't know," she responds.

I sigh and let out a long breath. I don't know what to do. I am desperate to know how the surgery has gone but am terrified of upsetting Mum and incurring her wrath.

"Shall I phone Jane?" I ask. "Just to let her know there is no news yet."

I remind Mum that time is getting on and I'm sure Dad should be out of theatre by now. Mum says she will phone the hospital again so I dial the number for her and for a second time get through to the High Dependency Unit. This time Mum lets me speak to the nurse and after giving my dad's details I am concerned to hear that they have no such patient of that name. I ask where else my dad might have gone and she suggests I try the Intensive Care Unit. This I do and am met with the same response.

I am becoming increasingly worried and I realise I am trembling as I call Eleanor to tell her what I know, or more to the point, what I don't know. I am about to suggest that Eleanor should phone as she will be able to speak more freely from her own home when she interrupts, saying without hesitation, "I'm going down there."

I confirm I will get Mum ready and we will also go to the hospital; it is almost 6.00pm and the absence of information is causing bewilderment and despair. I call Jane to let her know we are on our way to the hospital and she asks us to pick her up.

I phone for a taxi and soon we are walking through the hospital having decided to go back to the ward which Dad had been on prior to his surgery. We don't know where else to go and although I never expected for a moment that Dad would still be there, I was sure someone would know where he was.

The three of us arrive at the ward and go straight to the nurses' station. I give my dad's name and a nurse asks who we are. We are then ushered into a room just outside the ward and the nurse says, "Someone will be along in a minute." The door remains open and Eleanor and her husband Jack, walk by. I call them into the room and they are followed immediately by the ward sister.

She speaks directly to my mum, asking her whether she understands what Dad is in for. Mum responds, "Yes, he has got cancer." She does not say anymore and the room falls silent for the longest moment. The ward sister explains that Dad had been taken into theatre but the proposed procedure could not be carried out and instead Dad has been fitted with a colostomy bag and made comfortable. He is back on this ward where he will remain.

We are all speechless. I turn to Mum and Eleanor takes her hand. Mum appears nonplussed while the rest of us are in a state of shock. Jane stammers, "Why, what's wrong, what's wrong, where is Dad?"

Eleanor, Jack and I remained silent; eventually the sister tells us that the consultant would speak to us in the morning adding that Dad was in the same place as he was in previously and we could go in to see him, although he was still asleep following the procedure so we should only stay for a short while.

We stand around Dad's bed in stunned silence. He is in a deep sleep and unaware of our presence. I think none of us knows what to say; we do not know why the proposed surgery has not taken place but I think we all understand that it cannot be good news.

We leave after a while and still we have hardly spoken.

I go back to Mum's house and go to bed fairly early; it has been a truly difficult day and I for one am exhausted. After a restless night, I get up to make myself a cup of tea at around 6:00am. Mum is snoring gently and I am grateful that she is getting some rest.

I sit in the dark with my tea and wonder what today has in store for us. I think I must have been numb at this point because I don't remember feeling afraid or worried. I only remember sitting there with my hands wrapped around my cup, staring at nothing in particular.

I hear Mum moving around upstairs and I press the button on my speaking clock which tells me it is eight thirty-five. I go upstairs to find Mum wandering around her room looking for her clothes.

"I'll help you," I tell her as I hand Mum her dressing gown, adding, "Shall we go down and have some breakfast before we get dressed?"

The phone rings whilst we are still in the bedroom and Mum answers.

"Yes, speaking," she responds to the caller. After a moment she says, "OK Doctor I will be there, thank you." The receiver is replaced.

I hold my breath and wait for Mum to speak. To my surprise she says, "That was your Dad's doctor, he wants to see us at ten o'clock this morning."

"Oh," is all I manage to say.

I let Eleanor and Jane know about the meeting and at nine fifty we are all at the nurses' station once again.

A nurse says the consultant will be along to see us shortly and once more we are ushered into the relatives' room. My heart is racing at this point – my mouth is dry and I am beginning to tremble. It wouldn't take much to have me wailing in fear and it takes a monumental effort to remain composed. Mum is holding my arm as we enter the room and we both sit at one end of a small row of chairs. The consultant, Mr Baker, sits perpendicular to Mum on her left and Jane sits on my right with tears in her eyes; Jack and Eleanor sit opposite the consultant who introduces himself and asks whether we are all Dennis's family.

Jack, who can always be relied upon to lighten even the darkest moment tells the consultant, "this is Dennis's three daughters and I am his favourite son-in-law."

The softly-spoken consultant, who we had first met a few weeks ago at an outpatient's appointment to discuss Dad's surgery, asks Mum whether she understands what is wrong with Dad. She responds, "Yes, he has cancer and is here for an operation to sort it out."

The rest of us remain silent. I am desperate to know what is going on and at the same time dread hearing what the consultant has to tell us.

He seems to draw in his breath and says, "When we got Dennis into theatre, it became apparent that the tumour was far larger and more widespread than any of the tests had revealed."

I am fairly close to him and can make out his gestures as he indicates the top of his left leg saying, "The tumour is touching a major blood vessel at the top of the leg. It is also touching his stomach wall. It does not appear to have spread into any major organs at this stage but the size and proximity of the tumour makes it impossible to remove."

The room falls silent for ages and we are asked whether we have any questions. Again, we are inaudible for the longest time and although I have formulated the question in my mind, I do not want to verbalise it. I wait for the consultant to speak and when he remains silent, I ask, "So how long?" I stammer. "How long before it's …" My words trail away. I do not know how to ask the question to which I dread the answer.

Mr Baker's words break into the silence. "Weeks, perhaps months, but not years."

Jane lets out a shriek. "No, please no," she cries.

Eleanor asks whether Dad is aware of the situation.

"Yes," comes the response. "I spoke with Dennis this morning; he expressed concerns about his family but otherwise said very little."

How typical of Dad I think. Never one to make a fuss. Jane is sobbing quietly. Mum has said very little and Mr Baker says Dad is awake and we can go in to see him, although we should not stay too long as he is very tired and the best thing for him at the moment is to rest.

We sit around Dad's bed for a while. I have to breathe deeply just to stop the tears flowing – there will be plenty of time for that later. Right now I just want things to be as normal as possible. Normal! Who am I kidding, things will never be normal again.

4

MUM'S DIAGNOSIS

Dad is eventually discharged on 6 January after almost four weeks in hospital. Christmas Day is spent with us all around Dad's bed and we take in presents as we try to make the best of the day. Dad is feeling a whole lot better by this time and is sitting in a chair at the side of his bed. The other four patients who have been in the ward with him were discharged a couple of days earlier and it is nice to have the space to ourselves so that we can enjoy the chat and laughter which always accompanies our get-togethers. OK, the sadness is never far below the surface but it is great to see Dad looking so well and enjoying the camaraderie and exchanging of presents. It was only yesterday that a tube had been removed from Dad's nose which went into his stomach to help alleviate the constant vomiting he has suffered over the previous five days.

Christmas Day that year is as good as it can be. I would go so far as to say that, taking everything into account, it is pretty wonderful! Like I said, Dad is in really good fettle and this lifts our spirits no end. There was a time shortly after the consultant delivered the shattering news just nine days ago that Dad only had weeks to live, when I thought we would be attending Dad's funeral between Christmas and New Year.

As well as the constant vomiting which caused Dad a lot of discomfort and worry, last week we had been told Dad was under a kidney specialist as there were signs of problems with his kidneys which were giving medical staff cause for concern. However, when we visited on Christmas Eve we were told the kidney specialist is now happy as Dad's kidneys are functioning well. We could not have asked for a more precious Christmas gift.

Just before Dad is discharged, I decide to return to my home in Scotland for a little while. I have been staying at Mum and Dad's house since early December and I know that both Eleanor and Jane are concerned about me being away from home for so long. Dad too assures me that he is looking forward to going home and implores me to go home also for a few days so that, in his words, I can have a bit of a rest.

Although I am reluctant to do so, Eleanor assures me she will stay with Mum until Dad gets out of hospital and then she and Jane will visit Mum and Dad every day. I have to admit to feeling glad to be back in my own home for a while although my dad is never far from my thoughts and I often find myself bursting into tears, which is something I have done my best to suppress when I am with Mum.

I return to Mum and Dad's house around 10 January and stay for a week, during which time Dad ventures out for the first time since his discharge. We also celebrate Eleanor's birthday on 13 January and it is lovely to have this time together.

Dad's first venture out of the house was to his beloved Royal Naval Association, (RNA) club. He is one of the founder members of the club and he loves going there on a Thursday afternoon which was specifically for those members over 65, where he would enjoy a pint and a game of bingo. Mum would tease him about this saying, "Are you going to your geriatric bingo today?"

I decide to accompany Dad to the club where he is greeted by a small group of friends who are glad to see him after his lengthy absence. Dad is animated whilst with his friends and it is lovely to see him doing something he really enjoys.

I take the opportunity to do a bit of shopping whilst Dad plays bingo. I go into a card shop to get cards for Eleanor's birthday; one from me and one from Mum and Dad as Dad is not up to shopping and Mum would probably not remember that her oldest daughter's birthday was only days away.

I ask an assistant to help me find the relevant cards and when I mention a 'Daughter' card, a lump comes to my throat as I realise this will be the last birthday card Eleanor will receive from Dad. I am overwhelmed with sadness. At the same time, an enormous sense of joy that we are to have this celebration as a family lifts my spirits no end.

Once again I return to my own home for a few days and during this period I speak with my sisters every day – they are becoming increasingly concerned about Mum's health. She is becoming more and more confused, with episodes of ill temper and aggression towards each of them.

I decide to return to Mum and Dad's home and anticipate a prolonged visit this time. I am ill at ease when I am back in Scotland, and feel helpless being so far away from my sisters who seem to be bearing the brunt of Mum's bizarre behaviour.

Sometime around late January I return to my parent's home.

Dad is doing quite well. He goes to his beloved RNA club now and again but for the most part he just enjoys reading his morning paper and spending time with 'his girls', as we are known. Both my sisters visit every day and their children are also frequent visitors.

Eleanor and Jane have become so worried and disturbed by Mum's strange behaviour of late that they have spoken to her GP who has assured them he would contact a specialist and try to get someone to come to the house to see Mum.

The GP of course is familiar with my dad's recent diagnosis and, seeing the distress and anxiety of Eleanor and Jane, decides that the matter requires a degree of urgency. Jane receives a phone call the day after her meeting with the GP to confirm that a doctor will call to see my mum in a few days' time.

The morning of the visit arrives. All three of us agree to be at the house when the doctor comes. Dad is aware of what is going on. He is concerned that we are going behind Mum's back but agrees that something has to be done as Mum's behaviour is becoming increasingly erratic and worrying.

Mum and Dad have just finished breakfast when there is a knock at the door. I open it to Eleanor and she walks past me proclaiming, "I feel sick."

"So do I," is my response.

Mum is in the kitchen and Dad is in his usual armchair. My stomach is in knots. I am starving but the thought of eating anything makes me feel nauseous. Jane arrives shortly after and she is equally harrowed and afraid. I told Mum earlier that morning that a doctor was coming to the house. She asked why as the district nurses were coming in to see Dad so why was a doctor coming as well? Dad isn't unwell today so why did he need a doctor she wanted to know.

"I think he is just coming to see how you are both coping, he wants to see you as well," I say and hold my breath in anticipation of a rant. Mum seems to accept this without further question and whilst I am relieved at her capitulation, I feel wretched at the deceit and duplicity and inwardly beg forgiveness, from where I am not really sure.

The appointment time is drawing near and the monumental effort to maintain an air of calm and normality is taking its toll on me. I am running to the bathroom every few minutes and the nervous energy has me rushing around like a dervish. I just want the visit to be over but am terrified of the consequences. We have all incurred Mum's wrath over the last couple of months which in itself is upsetting but when her outbursts are directed towards Dad, who is just too weak to withstand what we are all witnessing, we know something has to be done.

The dreaded knock comes, right on time. I go to answer it proclaiming, "This will be the doctor," trying to inject a modicum of normality which I certainly don't feel, into my voice.

Introductions are made; the doctor advises he is Mr Addlington from the Cherry Tree. This means nothing to any of us – we are not familiar with the Cherry Tree at this time. We will, however, soon come to be regular visitors to the geriatric psychiatric day centre which is situated in this abode.

All five of us are in the lounge and Mr Addlington suggests that perhaps Mum and Dad might like to sit at the table in the kitchen so that he can have a chat with them both. He gestures that I should join them whilst Eleanor and Jane remain in the lounge. I must admit to feeling quite a bit better at this point. Mr Addlington seems to exude an air of calm and Mum seems relaxed and accepting of his presence, which is a huge relief.

Mum is soon engaged in a conversation with Mr Addlington and shortly he asks her whether she would mind answering some particular questions. Mum mumbles something along the lines of, "What's the point of all this?" Nevertheless she acquiesced.

Some papers are produced and Mum's first assessment begins. It all sounds really bizarre to me and I get the feeling that Dad too is a bit puzzled. I squeeze Dad's hand gently to try and offer some comfort and reassurance that all is OK, even though I feel anything but.

Mr Addlington thanks Mum and suggests she goes into the lounge whilst he has a quick word with Dad and me. Again, Mum mutters something as she gets up from the table but thankfully her tone is light and once again she appears remarkably accepting of the situation.

Mr Addlington makes a few notes and asks us about Mum's behaviour and her reaction to Dad's cancer diagnosis. We chat for a while. Dad gets really upset as he tries to explain that he does not think Mum will be able to cope on her own. He thinks she may need to go into a care home. A lump forms in my throat at Dad's words as I realise that he is not only dealing with his own illness, he is worrying about what will happen to Mum when he is no longer here to care for her; I can't speak for a moment. I desperately want to give Dad some words of comfort and at the same time I have an overwhelming urge to go and put my arms around Mum as I realise what impact Dad's death will have upon her.

Mr Addlington's voice interrupts my thoughts as he tells us he thinks Mum is probably in the early stage of Alzheimer's, although his assessment has not been as thorough as he would have liked bearing in mind Dad's illness and the fact that Mum is blind and therefore not able to participate in one aspect of the assessment. He tells us he will speak to the Community Psychiatric Nurse (CPN) who will contact us shortly with a view to visiting Mum in the near future.

Mr Addlington leaves details of the Cherry Tree, advising that it is located in the grounds of Aintree University Hospital and we should not hesitate to contact them, or even pay a visit should we wish to talk to someone about Mum's diagnosis.

Dad thanks the doctor and he leaves, telling Dad and I that we should not hesitate to contact his secretary if we have any further concerns and confirmed that once a CPN has been allocated to Mum, we will have a specific point of contact with whom to liaise.

5

HE WAS CRYING

I am back at home for a few days after a lengthy spell at Mum and Dad's house and must admit to feeling relieved at a break from the overwhelming sadness and despair I feel when I see what is happening to my parents. Even though I will speak to them regularly and my sisters will let me know how they are doing, there is a part of me that feels guilty for relishing these few days at my own home.

Dad has been up and down over recent weeks and even has the occasional day when he seems so well it is hard to believe just how ill he is. These are the days we relish and simply enjoy being around Dad; we know such days will become less frequent and want to make the most of the good times.

There are times when Dad does not have the energy to get out of his chair although he always insists that as long as he can get out of bed every day and put his feet on the floor, he will be quite happy. These days, Mum and I get him washed and dressed and then help him as he makes his way downstairs into his favourite armchair. He loves to read his morning paper so either me or one of my sisters go to the local shop to get this for him.

After several consecutive good days Eleanor wonders whether he is in remission; she is quite excited at the prospect proclaiming, “The doctors don’t always get it right.”

I, however, have my doubts as my understanding of a cancer patient in remission is when a particular course of treatment has proved successful at halting the disease but not eliminating it and, apart from pain relief, Dad is receiving no treatment. I don’t share my thoughts with Eleanor as I do not want to shatter her hopes.

The day after I arrive home I decide to go into Glasgow with Stewart; I hope a spot of lunch and change of scene will take my mind off things. Whilst out, Eleanor phones to say Dad had phoned her shortly after I had left and asked her if she would come to stay with him. Eleanor becomes upset when she explains that Dad had been crying as he told her, “I don’t want to be on my own with Mum, I am frightened.”

Any appetite I may have has disappeared and the familiar tightening in my throat to stem the flow of tears hits me like a blow to the solar plexus as it has so many times since Dad’s diagnosis.

We return home immediately and I prepare to travel the two hundred miles back to my parent’s home. During my journey Eleanor phones to let me know Dad is a lot calmer, but it is evident that he does not want her to leave. After spending the night and most of that morning at Mum and Dad’s house she had suggested that she would go out for a short while, thinking that they would like some time to themselves; however Dad had become distressed and breathless. Eleanor immediately took off her coat and assured Dad she was going nowhere.

I arrive a few hours later and Eleanor explains that Dad has told her Mum's behaviour has been giving him cause for concern and he is not well enough to cope by himself. He is afraid to be alone with her as she has become erratic and unpredictable and is sometimes aggressive towards him.

Eleanor, Jane and I decide that from now on, one of us will stay at the house day and night. Up until this time we have been visiting every day, tending to all their needs and ensuring all Dad's medication is in order and the cooking and cleaning is kept up-to-date and so on. We had thought that they would prefer to be left alone occasionally but it now appears this is the last thing Dad wants.

The next few weeks see Dad deteriorate quite considerably whilst Mum appears to be up and down with mood swings which are so bizarre it is hard to know what to expect from one minute to the next.

I remember the time just a couple of weeks before the proposed surgery when Dad was to see the consultant, it was 29 November by which time all of the test results were available. This time, Mum had decided to accompany Dad and me, and both my sisters also went along. I went in to see the consultant with Mum and Dad. After introductions the consultant, Mr Baker, told us, "The bad news is," I held my breath as he continued, "you do have cancer in your bowel; the good news is, it does not appear to have spread anywhere else."

I sighed with relief. As far as I knew, the cancer diagnosis delivered by the nurse three weeks ago was not in any doubt, but looking back on that meeting with Mr Baker, I realise that we were just having everything confirmed following the myriad of tests over recent weeks.

The rest of that meeting was a bit of a haze but I remember Mum asking something, I can't remember what, but whatever it was Dad was prompted to say to the consultant, "my wife gets a bit confused." To my surprise the response came, "Yes, I can see that."

I wonder whether after the briefest encounter with my Mum, the consultant had picked up on something being not quite right with her. Mum seemed oblivious to the exchange.

Mr Baker told Dad he would arrange for the operation to take place within the next two weeks and a nurse would be along shortly to explain more about the procedure. He left then, telling Dad, "I'll see you in theatre."

I slipped outside to tell my sisters what had been discussed and then went back into the room just ahead of the nurse. She explained the procedure and said Dad may require a bit of chemo after the operation but that would just be the 'icing on the cake.' She actually used that cliché and it made me think, things are not too terrible, they seem to have everything under control. I left the hospital feeling a whole lot better than when I entered it thinking, things were not so bad; for the first time in weeks I felt optimistic about the future. The thought of losing Dad was unbearable but now I felt like I could smile again in the belief that Dad was going to be fine.

I had had two concerns before seeing the consultant, the obvious one being that the tests would reveal the cancer had spread elsewhere; my other concern was that Dad's longstanding heart condition would make the surgical procedure too risky but neither of my concerns seemed to be an issue which was a huge relief.

6

BROKEN

"How the hell did she manage to break the toilet?" It's Eleanor, who is doing nothing to disguise her frustration, as I try to explain that we need to get hold of a plumber right away to install a new one. It can no longer be flushed.

"How did she do it?" demands Eleanor.

"It doesn't matter how she did it, we need to get it sorted right away." My own tone is bordering on hostile and I have to reign in my frustration as the last thing we need right now is for my sisters and I to fall out.

"Isn't there a small plumber's merchant at the end of your road?" I ask. "Can you go up there and see if they can help; we need a new toilet and someone to install it."

Eleanor agrees to go to the plumbers and promises to call back shortly.

A day or so before Dad was discharged from hospital, we had a visit from a social worker who explained she had been contacted by the hospital and was here to see what Dad may need once he came home. Later that day, to my surprise, a delivery of a frame arrived which was designed to raise the level of the toilet seat. The contraption was placed over the entire toilet and had rails at either side to allow the user some support.

Upon seeing the frame in situ I thought there would be no benefit to Dad as he was now using a colostomy bag and therefore, not to put too fine a point on it, would not need to sit on the toilet. Nevertheless, I told myself they must know what they were doing and was grateful that Dad was on the radar and it surely meant we would not be alone once he came home. This gave me an enormous sense of comfort and I felt safe in the knowledge that help would always be just a phone call away.

Although Mum was present when the contraption was installed and seemed to accept its presence, the first time she encountered it she was confused and demanded to know what the hell was this thing doing over the toilet? I reminded her about the social worker's visit and tried to explain that it was to make things a bit easier for Dad when he came home. I left her to it and to my horror, as I walked downstairs, I heard Mum muttering and cursing and then what I can only describe as some rattling and banging coming from the bathroom, I returned to find Mum hauling and yanking at the contraption which in turn was clattering against the cistern.

"Mum, Mum don't do that," I chastised as I tried to calm her and explained once again the reason for the frame. Mum seemed to accept this and after a little while I heard the toilet being flushed and presently Mum joined me back downstairs.

Later that day another delivery arrived. This time it was a seat to be used across the bath so that Dad could get in and out of it without too much difficulty. This time however, upon seeing the type of bath in the house, it became apparent that the seat was not designed to fit the style of bath which was a bit old-fashioned having, been installed in the Eighties.

The seat was taken away with the news that there probably wouldn't be anything available to suit that style of bath. Nevertheless I still felt confident that we would get all the help we required to meet Dad's needs.

Over the coming weeks, when all of our energy and focus was concentrated on catering for all of Dad's requirements, Mum seemed to be drifting between lucidity and confusion with her frustration increasingly being metered out on the contraption in the bathroom.

Mum seemed to do battle with the contraption at least once a day – she would shake and haul at the 'bloody nuisance' as she referred to it and I thought it would only be a matter of time before it, or the toilet, were permanently damaged.

Following my call to Eleanor, Mum demands to know what we have been talking about. I remind her that the toilet is broken. I don't dare tell her she was the one who has broken it. She immediately leaps to her feet and goes to the phone, dials Directory Enquiries and asks to be connected to the local builders and plumbers merchant. I hear one side of a conversation which culminates in Mum giving her name and address adding, "Yes OK you can come out to measure up next week."

"Mum, what was that all about?" I ask.

"I am sorting it!" she says. "We need a new toilet and someone will be out next week to measure up."

I sigh in frustration. "That's no use Mum." I try to keep my tone gentle but what I really want to do is scream at her to let me get on with it. "We don't need measuring up for a whole new bathroom; we just need a toilet and we need it now."

Dad is dozing in his chair and for the time being is unaware of the problem.

Eventually Eleanor calls and confirms she has managed to get hold of a plumber who will deliver and fit the new toilet later on this afternoon. I breathe a sigh of relief and decide I will deal with Mum's rebuke later. By the time the plumber arrives she may well have forgotten all about the problem.

The rest of the day passes with no additional outrage from Mum and the new toilet is fitted without further incident.

When I realise how easily the contraption has been removed from the broken toilet, I wish I had removed the bloody thing weeks ago and saved us all a whole lot of bother! Needless to say, it did not go back onto the new toilet.

7

CUP OF TEA

JANE'S STORY

It's Sunday morning and I am on the phone to Eleanor. She tells me that Dad is not very well today. Eleanor has been staying with Mum and Dad since Friday morning when Liz went home for a few days.

I tell her I will be up shortly as I know she wants to go into town to meet Jack so they can have lunch together. Eleanor will be staying at Mum and Dad's house for a few more days until Liz comes back.

I feel bad that I cannot do more to help but I know that I cannot stay with them overnight; I am afraid of Mum and I know that if she gets really angry and throws me out, I will just go and leave Dad alone with her. This would be the worst thing I could do as I know that Dad too is afraid of Mum when she slips into one of her moods. Although we have all come to realise that it is not her fault, it does not make things any easier.

Dad's illness and his needs are forever at the forefront of my mind and I do not seem to have room in my head for anything else.

Mum's indifference and apathy toward Dad is heart-breaking to witness as, before Mum's illness, they had enjoyed a very happy and loving life together; Mum could not do enough for Dad whenever he was a bit under the weather.

I remember when Dad suffered his first heart attack in February 1991. Mum was the perfect doting wife and looked after Dad throughout his recovery, giving up her own social activities so that Dad was never left at home by himself. At that time Mum attended a social group for blind people twice a week and although Dad insisted that she continue with this, she was determined to remain at home with him. She never returned to this, even when Dad was well and truly back on his feet.

When I arrive at Mum and Dad's house Eleanor tells me she has cooked the dinner and all that needs to be done is to make gravy and serve the meal as soon as they are ready to eat.

I sit in Dad's usual armchair; he is sitting on the couch. I ask him how he is and he tells me he is just a bit tired but I can tell from his voice that he is far from OK. Mum sits in silence and her demeanour tells me she is in a mood – she has not spoken to me since I arrived and this in itself is more telling than anything. Mum's usual greeting when any of her family visits is warm and welcoming.

I make small talk with Mum but I know for sure that she is in one of her moods. I know this is the wrong term as a mood is something that you can bring yourself out of whereas Mum cannot do anything about it.

I ask whether anyone wants a cuppa and make a tea for Mum and coffee for Dad. The tension in the room is palpable and I just sit there with a dreadful sense of foreboding. Mum sits and drinks her tea and she seems oblivious of Dad's suffering. I wonder how she can be so horrible when Dad is so ill but we are only just learning about Alzheimer's and are ignorant of how this devastating disease can completely transform its host so cruelly. All we can focus upon is Dad's terminal cancer.

After a while of Mum demanding to know what is coming on telly this afternoon and insisting that Dad reads the telly page as well as telling him to go and make her a cup of tea, it is apparent that Mum's mood is not getting any better and when she says she is ready for her lunch, I go into the kitchen to serve it when I hear, in a tone which makes my blood run cold, "Jane, get back in here and let that lazy git do it, he has sat on his bloody arse all day and I have not stopped at all!"

My stomach falls to the floor but I just go back into the lounge and sit down. After I don't know how long I tiptoe back into the kitchen and hear the same again from Mum.

"Get back in here!" she shouts.

I return and sit down but I can feel Dad's anxiety mounting. This happens a couple more times with the same result. Dad eventually gets up from the couch with an enormous effort and makes his way into the kitchen but just stands, leaning against the worktop. The effort of getting up and walking the few steps into the kitchen had absolutely floored him. Once again I creep into the kitchen to help Dad who by this time is breathless and I fear he is about to collapse. I realise that Dad has been trying to get into the cupboard for a saucepan and the effort of bending down has proved too difficult for him.

Fortunately, Mum does not demand that I come in from the kitchen –perhaps she is just satisfied that he is in there doing something.

I put the meal out whilst Dad just leans against the worktop. Mum comes in and eats her lunch. (I cannot remember whether Dad ate anything that day). He makes his way back into the lounge and sits on the couch. Mum finishes her meal and returns to the lounge while I started clearing things away in the kitchen. Mum seems content to let me do this and I am relieved to hear nothing from her.

Eleanor arrives back. She asks how things are and I explain what has happened. Eleanor is furious and storms into see Mum, asking, "What do you think you're playing at when Dad is so ill?"

Mum shouts at Eleanor, "Get the hell out of my house!"

Eleanor responds, "I am not going anywhere, I am staying here to look after Dad."

"I can look after your father," Mum screams. "I have done so for the past fifty bloody years and I will do it now!"

The exchange is witnessed by Dad, who eventually struggles to get up from the couch, and makes his way into the kitchen. Eleanor realises how the exchange has upset Dad and she immediately calms down in an attempt to placate Mum. I return to the lounge and sit in the chair opposite Mum whilst Eleanor tries to comfort Dad.

At this moment Mum throws her cup of tea at Eleanor but as she has just moved the hot liquid hits me full in the face. I sit frozen in complete shock and then I hear what I can only describe as a whale-like sound coming from the kitchen. It was Dad and I realise that he has witnessed what Mum has done. I run and put my arms around him and sob through my pain.

"It's alright Dad, I am OK; I just got a bit of a fright."

I stand there with Dad for a couple of minutes and I can hear Eleanor telling Mum what she has done and how it has upset Dad.

Mum asks me, "Did that get you?"

"Yes," I say, "but I am alright."

"Sorry," Mum says, "it was meant for the other one," gesturing towards where she thinks Eleanor is.

Eleanor goes upstairs where she phones Jack to tell him what has happened. Jack suggests that we should call the district nurses to check that Dad is OK and said he will come up to see if there is anything he can do to help.

Jack arrives shortly and he sits beside Mum who seems to be a bit calmer by this time and is sitting on the couch beside Dad.

"Oh good," Mum proclaims, "Have you come to take that one home?"

"No" Jack responds, "Eleanor has to stay here to help you look after Dennis, he is not very well."

Mum huffs and puffs but otherwise says nothing. Dad seems to be calming down a bit and the room is silent for a few moments.

There is a knock at the door. Eleanor and I both go to answer it and, as expected, it is the district nurses. I explain the events of the last few hours and say that both Mum and Dad seem to be a lot calmer.

One of the nurses asks whether they should go in to see Dad, suggesting that if all is calm at the moment, it may be best not to disturb him as their presence may only serve to annoy Mum.

I am in a quandary as I had been so worried about Dad earlier. Once again the nurse who has spoken says it will probably be best if they do not come in and assure us that we can call them back if we become concerned again later. Eleanor and I agree that the nurse's suggestion is probably for the best and they leave shortly thereafter.

8

HEART ATTACK

It is almost three weeks since the day Mum threw a cup of tea at Jane. I travel to Mum and Dad's house the following day after hearing about this distressing incident. I am determined that, on this occasion, I will remain there indefinitely. Dad is becoming increasingly weak and even though I do not want to voice my fears, I am sure he is nearing the end of his life.

My other concern is the dramatic change in Mum's condition; it is obvious that we have to do our best to look after Dad whilst giving Mum as much help and support as she needs.

Thankfully, there are no further incidents like the one on that awful Sunday afternoon and the intervening weeks are spent in relative peace with a heavy cloak of sadness and fear forever present.

On Friday 7 April a noticeable change occurs in Dad's condition He really seems to be struggling; he has barely left his armchair and has little appetite, even refusing a cup of coffee. His morning paper lies untouched and he keeps drifting in and out of sleep.

"Are you OK Dad?" I ask.

"Just a bit tired today," he responds.

I am really worried as he seems to have deteriorated overnight and I ask him whether he wants me to phone a doctor, or perhaps ask the district nurse to call.

"No, I will be alright after a bit of a doze," he insists, but I know that he is more than just tired. As is always the way with Dad, he does not want to make a fuss.

Eleanor and Jane are both on their way. Jane did have other plans for today but when she phoned this morning to see how Mum and Dad are, she immediately cancelled upon learning that Dad is not too good. Eleanor is here every day and will be here as usual this afternoon.

I have noticed that Dad is absently rubbing his left thigh and I ask whether he has a pain there. When the consultant spoke to us in December to explain why the cancer was inoperable, he described the tumour in his bowel as being very large and close to a major blood vessel at the top of his left leg. I do not know whether Dad was made aware of this and indeed he has never complained of any problem with his leg, but this rubbing which is a new thing, has me worried.

Jane arrives and I make some tea and soup for lunch. I ask Dad whether he wants help into the kitchen but he says he does not feel like anything to eat and remains in his chair.

Eleanor comes with her youngest daughter Jade who is newly qualified as a nurse and her presence offers me some comfort. I ask her how she thinks Dad looks today.

"Just really tired," she responds.

Maybe I am over-reacting but I can't help thinking that he has reached a new phase of his illness and I am filled with foreboding.

Mum is in a world of her own today. She does not seem to be aware of Dad's lethargy, asking him to go and make her a cup of tea and telling him not to be so lazy – totally out of character for Mum as when she is 'herself' she cannot do enough for Dad.

I ask Mum whether she wants to go to Iris's for a little while. I know it really upsets Dad to see mum's condition transform her from the person he has known and loved for fifty-two years into this unrecognisable presence in his life. Dad understands that Mum has Alzheimer's and I know he fears for her future when he is no longer around to look after her.

Mum agrees to go into her sister's house so Eleanor takes her in and sits for a while, telling Iris how Dad is today; she leaves mum with Iris and returns to Mum and Dad's house. The five of us sit quietly. Dad does not seem to have the energy to talk and to be honest, I don't think any of us know what to say, we are all lost in our own thoughts. Jane gets up saying she needs the toilet but I know she has gone upstairs to have a cry. I hear her sniffles as she leaves the room.

It's 5:00pm and apart from a few sips of water with his medication, Dad has had nothing to eat or drink today. The phone rings and when I answer I hear Iris ask if someone will come and take Mum home as she is getting a bit agitated. I immediately go and collect mum. She doesn't ask about Dad, instead she tells me to put the kettle on and asks what we are having for tea.

"There is a cooked chicken in the fridge and some salad, shall we have that with some new potatoes?" I ask.

"That sounds nice," she says. "When will it be ready?"

We sit around the table but again Dad says he doesn't want anything. I make him a sandwich with some of the chicken and take it to him with a cup of coffee. I do not ask whether he wants it; I just place it on the small table beside his armchair and say, "there you are," in the hope that he will at least have a nibble at it.

Eleanor and Jane go home around 7:00pm. I had previously asked Jade whether she would spend the night and she had agreed. Eleanor makes me promise to call her if I feel Dad gets any worse and confirms she will come straight back, otherwise she will be back in the morning.

To my surprise and delight, Dad finishes the sandwich I have made and then says he wants to go to bed. Jade helps me to get Dad upstairs but he is struggling to reach the top. It takes ages. He has to stop after every two or three steps, holding onto the handrail to steady himself and I am so grateful that Jade is here to help me. There are times when I think Dad could have easily toppled backwards, such is his difficulty and even though Jade and I are close behind, I fear we will be unable to hold him should he fall.

Eventually we manage to help Dad to the bedroom; he sits on the bed and asks me whether I would help him empty his colostomy bag.

"Of course I will Dad, just let me get the bits and bobs together."

It really upsets me that Dad feels he needs to ask me to do this for him. I have been performing this task with him for the past few weeks and there is no way I will not do it but he always seems to be apologetic at having to ask.

I use a small bucket with a tight lid to empty the bag into, the contents of which are immediately diluted with water and a large amount of Dettol. The routine is for me to then take the bucket into the bathroom and tip its contents down the toilet, clean it out then put fresh water and Dettol into it and put it back beside the bed in case Dad feels the need to empty his bag again during the night.

Just as I am finishing this task and Dad is settled in bed, Mum comes upstairs demanding to know what we are all up to.

"It's OK Mum," I say, "Dad is in bed; he seems to be really tired and is almost asleep."

"What's he doing in bed already?" Mum exclaims, "It's far too early."

"I think he's just a bit tired Mum."

I try to reassure her that there's nothing to worry about but to be honest, she seems more angry than worried and I'm afraid she might disturb Dad, such is her frame of mind. She is in the bedroom rummaging through a drawer, for what I don't know and when I ask if I can help she tells me to sod off downstairs, adding, "I can manage myself."

I am confident that Dad is settled so I leave Mum to it and go downstairs. Jade makes me a cup of tea and asks how things are.

"I don't know Jade, I just don't know, I don't know what to do,"" is all I can say as I sit with my head in my hands.

We all go to bed a short while later and I am woken from a restless sleep by movement in Mum and Dad's room. I go to the door where I realise Dad is sitting on the edge of the bed and is quite breathless. Mum is snoring and I ask Dad whether he needs anything.

"It's OK," he responds, "I just need to empty this bag."

Once again I fetch the bucket, wipes and spray and go through the well-practised ritual. Dad gets back into bed and assures me he is OK, telling me I should go back to bed and try to get some sleep. I take the bucket into the bathroom but I am so exhausted I just clean my hands and go to bed. I will sort the bucket in the morning I tell myself.

I awake around 6:30am and hear Mum shuffling around in her room. Dad seems to be in a deep sleep and I hope Mum will not waken him.

"Shall we go down and have a cup of tea Mum?" I ask quietly.

"Let's go," she says as I hand her dressing gown to her.

We sit at the kitchen table. Mum is eating cereal and hasn't said a word since we came downstairs. I have come to learn when Mum is in 'one of those moods' and I tiptoe around her lest I upset her. Jane is correct when she says these episodes are not 'moods' but it's hard to know how to think of these awful periods which take Mum away and leave behind someone who is unrecognisable to all of us.

I remember the bucket in the bathroom and go upstairs to clean it out. I am exhausted. I am so afraid for Dad and wonder what today will bring as I'm sure he has had a huge and sudden decline and simultaneously I am terrified of disturbing Mum and incurring her wrath. I know it is not her fault – she too is unwell and it's tearing me apart seeing my parents in such an awful state. Sometimes I just want to run away and leave it all behind.

My head aches and my throat hurts with the strain of holding back the sobs as I lift the bucket to empty its contents down the toilet. Too late I realise I did not tighten the lid properly during the night and as I go toward the toilet the bucket slips from my hands; I can only watch in disbelief and horror as the contents pool around my feet.

It all seems to happen in slow motion. I just stand there watching the contents of the bucket spread across the bathroom floor and I seem powerless to move. I stand looking down for the longest moment. My mind is blank as I stand there transfixed then, although inside my head I am screaming no, no, no, please for Christ sake no, not a sound comes from my mouth.

I compose myself (well, I say compose myself, looking back I don't remember a moment's composure throughout this devastating period of my life), anyway I remind myself there are things to be done. Dad is beginning to stir and I know he will get upset if he sees the state I have got myself into. I'm also afraid of Mum coming to investigate what is going on because I know with as much certainty as anyone can know the outcome of a future event, that if Mum is still in 'one of her moods' and I tell her what has happened, she will try to turf me out of the bathroom and insist on cleaning up the mess herself.

I call out to Jade. It is still only around 7:30am and she is fast asleep. I don't have to make too much noise in order to waken her and she immediately comes to my assistance.

"Oh God," she exclaims as she sees the mess on the floor. She immediately goes to fetch towels, poly bags, cleaning paraphernalia and between us we manage to get everything cleaned up.

It is later that morning after we have all had breakfast and Eleanor is sitting beside Dad on the couch, when Dad tells us he doesn't think he can manage the stairs anymore and asks us to arrange for a bed to be brought downstairs. Eleanor assures Dad we will get someone to help us bring the bed down and at this Mum exclaims, "What, bring a bed down here, no way, how am I supposed to make my way around with a bloody great bed to keep bumping into?"

Eleanor takes a deep breath and starts to tell Mum that Dad needs the bed downstairs. Her words trail away as Dad interrupts Eleanor, gesturing that we shouldn't talk about it just now. It is one of the most heartbreaking moments of my life. Dad is sitting on the couch like a little boy who has just been denied his favourite toy as Mum mutters to herself, oblivious of everything. Eleanor, Jane and I are silent and utterly bewildered at the impossible situation in which we find ourselves.

Once again we follow the well-practised ritual of tip-toeing around Mum whilst Dad can only watch in despair and helplessness.

Jane makes some tea and brings Mum a cake with her cuppa. Dad has a bit more of an appetite today but still he eats very little and seems every bit as weary as yesterday. Eleanor assures Dad that we will have a bed brought down into the lounge before bed-time. Dad barely registers her words. He seems so exhausted and I'm sure the distress of seeing Mum in such a state is taking its toll.

Eleanor asks Mum whether she would like to go to Iris's for a little while.

"No," she responds and her tone leaves no room for question.

As has happened numerous times over the past few months, all five of us sit not knowing what to say or do. I go into the kitchen so Dad cannot see me and my actions next bring meaning to the term 'falling apart'. I bend my knees and fold myself over, wrapping my arms around my lower legs in an attempt to hold myself together. I quite simply do not know what else to do.

When I return, Jane is on her way out with Mum and tells me they are going to see Iris for a little while.

"Try to stay out for as long as you can," I whisper to Jane. "We will get the bed down while Mum is not here."

By the time Mum returns, a single bed is in the alcove furthest away from her usual armchair. She, of course, is unaware of this and although we do not feel good about the deceit to which we are all party, we know there is no alternative. Dad needs the bed down here and his needs are paramount.

Eleanor and Jane eventually go home and once again make me promise to call them if Dad gets any worse, otherwise they will both be back in the morning. Mum goes to bed around 9:00pm and Dad and I watch a bit of telly. After helping Dad get into bed, I switch off the television and go upstairs and get myself ready for bed also. Although I am exhausted, I know I will hardly sleep. My bedroom door is left open as is the door into the lounge so that I will be able to hear Dad should he call on me.

I drift off and am awoken by Mum who is outside my room and shouting to Dad that he should switch that bloody telly off and come to bed. I go to her and coax her back into her room saying, "Dad is alright, he just can't manage the stairs so is sleeping downstairs, remember we brought a bed down for him this afternoon." I was relieved at Mum's acceptance of my words as she and I return to bed and it wasn't long before I hear gentle snoring coming from Mum's room.

I lie awake for the rest of the night, straining to listen for movement from Mum or Dad. I must have drifted off because I awake with a jolt by what I can only describe as thud, thud, thud. I am a bit disoriented and cannot make out what the sound is, nor where it comes from.

I quickly realise that Dad is in the hallway at the foot of the stairs and as I go to him I see he is holding his walking stick up toward the ceiling and it becomes apparent that he has used it to bang on the ceiling to attract my attention.

I feel a pang of despair when the events of yesterday come flooding back and am overwhelmed with sadness as I realise Dad doesn't have the energy to speak. I help him to his armchair where he sits for several moments trying to get his breath back and recover from the effort of walking the few steps from his bed into the hallway.

I phone both my sisters and suggest they come up straight away as I am terrified seeing Dad so weak and helpless. Dad eventually settles and tells me he is alright although I know that he is anything but.

Eleanor and Jane both arrive within half an hour by which time Mum has got up and is sitting eating her breakfast. I tell her I don't think Dad is too good today and I am going to call the district nurse. Mum seems disinterested and asks for some toast. Eleanor makes it whilst Jane sits beside Dad, trying to persuade him to try a bite to eat.

Dad manages a cup of coffee and Jane gives him some scrambled egg and a slice of bread which he makes an attempt at but only manages a little.

"I am going to call the district nurse," I tell Dad and to my surprise he simply says, "OK."

A couple of my nieces arrive while we are waiting for the nurse. It is getting on for midday and Jade makes some sandwiches for everyone. My sisters and nieces are sitting in the kitchen whilst Mum and Dad are in the lounge sitting quietly together. Mum doesn't say much and Dad is drifting in and out of sleep. There is a knock at the door which Jane answers. We are glad to see the nurse and after a brief chat with Dad, she goes to leave saying, "Your Dad just needs some rest," adding, "I will advise the regular nurse who has been attending your dad of your concerns."

Eleanor, Jane and I follow her out and we have a conversation at the end of the path out of Mum and Dad's hearing. I tell her there is a marked change in Dad's condition; he has little appetite and no longer has the energy to hold a conversation or walk a few steps. I am distressed whilst trying to explain the events of the last couple of days. The nurse assures us there is no need for concern at this stage and tells me I should go home to my own house and let Dad 'have a bit of peace'.

I cannot believe what I am hearing. I know Dad is really unwell and with Mum's condition becoming increasingly distressing I simply walk back into the house in floods of tears. I go straight upstairs as I do not want Dad to see me in such a state.

I am sitting on my bed not knowing what to do when Eleanor comes into my room and tells me that mum is once again muttering at dad.

As I write this, almost twelve years later, I can hardly believe my next words on that terrible day; my chest tightens and I clamp my teeth together whilst closing my eyes as if to distance myself from my thoughts. I spit out with an anger I did not know I possessed, "I fuckin' hate her." I collapsed into Eleanor's arms as the enormity of my words hit me and we both sit for many minutes just holding onto each other whilst we weep.

All is quiet downstairs. Jane is sitting with Mum and Dad whilst my nieces tidy up in the kitchen. One of them suggests that the three of us should go out for a bit while they are here to make sure Dad has whatever he needs. We reluctantly agree and we make our way to one of our cousins who lives close by.

We are gone for no more than half an hour when Molly phones and says, "You need to come back straight away, Grandad has asked for an ambulance."

We return immediately. Molly explains that Dad had told her he didn't know what was wrong but he thought he needed to be in hospital. We call an ambulance and when the two paramedics arrive, we tell them as much as possible about Dad's history and after asking Dad a few questions which he can barely answer, such is his state of exhaustion, he is taken into the ambulance accompanied by Eleanor whilst I, Jane, Molly and Mum follow with our cousin who had brought us back after Molly's call.

It's around 4:00pm and I am concerned to see how busy the A&E is. I hope Dad will be given some priority. Dad has already been put in a cubicle awaiting examination so Eleanor takes Mum in to sit beside him. Eleanor remains with them both, only to be told that she will have to wait outside in the waiting area as there is no room for two people to be in with Dad. Eleanor explains that my Mum is blind and very confused so could not be left alone with Dad but nevertheless she is told she cannot stay.

The rest of us remain in the waiting area for a short while, then Jane goes to make sure Mum is OK. Our main concern is that a doctor will come to see Dad and Mum will not be able to explain properly what is wrong. Before long, Jane comes out with Mum as Mum had asked for a cup of tea. Jane says she is going to stay with Dad whilst Eleanor and I look after Mum.

Molly fetches a cup of tea for Mum and for the moment she seems content to sit quietly drinking her tea.

We sit like this for more than an hour when Jane comes out telling us a nurse has been to see Dad and promises that a doctor will be in to see him very soon. I ask Mum whether she wants to go and sit with Dad to which she replies, "No, why can't I go home?"

After all the worry and despair I have felt for Dad over the last few days, I am suddenly hit by an enormous sense of sadness for my mum who does not seem to know where she is or what is going on.

It is around 7:30pm when Jack arrives. Molly goes home and asks us to phone her as soon as we have any news.

Jane is with Dad when the doctor visits him. She is advised that Dad has undergone an electrocardiogram (ECG) which has been repeated because the test had indicated Dad has suffered a heart attack although when asked, Dad states he feels no chest pain and this is causing some bewilderment to medical staff. A chest x-ray is also being organised as well as blood tests and we should know more once all the test results are available.

We sit about for several more hours, taking turns to be with Dad and eventually he is moved out of the cubicle in the A&E department and whilst still on a trolley is taken to a place which I can only describe as 'no-man's-land'. It is not exactly a corridor, but it is not exactly a ward, nor anything resembling a ward. It is just a large open space with a few plastic chairs and nothing much else.

Just before being moved the original doctor who has examined Dad and ordered the various tests said, "Your dad has suffered a heart attack and has a chest infection so he will be admitted for treatment."

Jane advises the doctor that Dad is on Morphine Sulphate tablets and the doctor suggests that this would probably explain the absence of chest pain.

We all wait around in no-man's-land for what seems like an eternity. Fortunately Dad is asleep for a while but Mum is becoming increasingly distressed and agitated, asking whether she can go to bed. I manage to find a comfortable armchair for her and I remain with her whilst the others are at Dad's bedside. There seems to be no sign of a bed on a ward becoming available any time soon and around 2:00am we are all back around Dad's bed. He is awake but very groggy. I am utterly exhausted and when Mum asks where she is and again asks whether she can go to bed, Dad says I should take Mum home and insists that Eleanor and Jane also go home and tried to get some sleep. It is the last thing I want to do but I know it is the best thing for Mum. She is exhausted and confused and I reluctantly phone a taxi to take us back to her house.

Eleanor and Jack promise to stay with Dad until he has been settled on a ward.

"Do you want a cup of tea Mum?" I ask as we get back to her house.

"Yes, is there anything to eat?"

I make some toast for the three of us and whilst we are eating the phone rings. It is Eleanor to let us know Dad is on a ward so she and Jack are on their way home. It is a huge relief to know that Dad is now settled and we finish our tea and toast and go to bed. It is around 3:00am and we are all thoroughly emotionally and physically drained.

9

YOU POOR THINGS

I am upstairs in Mum and Dad's bedroom so that I can make the phone call without Mum overhearing me. It does not sit well with me, all this sneaking around, but it is the only way my sisters and I are getting to know what is happening with Dad.

I get through to the Macmillan nurse who we met at an outpatient appointment Dad attended a couple of weeks ago. I want to let her know Dad has been admitted into hospital, she explains she has just been to the ward and spoken with Dad and was about to phone my mum.

I feel an enormous sense of relief at her words as Dad is being treated for a minor heart attack and chest infection and the medical staff caring for him appear to be paying no heed to the advanced stage of bowel cancer. Yes, we know there is nothing that can be done in relation to the cancer but it is comforting to know that the specialist nurse is now involved in Dad's care.

The nurse explains that the doctor is ready to discharge Dad however, she is not happy about this as, during her visit, Dad had become very upset saying, "I can't go home, can you find me somewhere to go?" Her words serve to silence me. I stuff my fist into my mouth to stop me from crying out, my throat constricts and the familiar pain around my jaw threatens to choke me as I fight back the sobs.

I explain that Mum has recently been diagnosed with Dementia and things at home are very difficult. Her immediate response is, "Oh you poor things, you are losing both your parents."

I hold my breath as I hear Mum coming up the stairs. Fortunately she goes into the bathroom, oblivious to me.

I wish the nurse had not said what she did. I remember thinking, that's stupid, Mum is just a bit forgetful and has mood swings, but that is just because of the dreadful sadness we all feel right now.

I ask how she thinks Dad is and she says, "He is very poorly."

Tentatively I ask whether she thinks Dad is nearing the end, to which she simply says, "Yes, I'm afraid he is."

She asks us to meet her the following afternoon and we finish the call.

I sit on the bed for a while wondering what to say to my mum and sisters who are both downstairs. Mum comes out of the bathroom and goes down. I follow her, trying not to let her know I am crying.

I tell Eleanor and Jane what the nurse has said about Dad not having much longer and Jane lets out a loud cry exclaiming, "No, no, please no!"

I take her hand and lead her to a chair and say as gently as I can, "come on, we knew this moment was coming."

Jane is shaking and I can do little to comfort her. Eleanor sits beside Mum who is in a world of her own and appears not to have heard the exchange. We tell Mum it is time to get ready for the evening visiting and she simply says, "OK let's go."

We sit around Dad's bed. He seems a bit better than the last few days and one of the nurses tells us Dad's chest infection is clearing up nicely, and says he is ready to be discharged. I do not mention to the nurse about my conversation earlier with the Macmillan nurse, preferring instead to wait until the meeting tomorrow when I hope we will get some positive news.

It is Thursday 13 April and tomorrow is Good Friday. I tell Dad I have spoken to the Macmillan nurse and we will be meeting her tomorrow when we come in for afternoon visiting. Dad appears to be glad to hear this and seems to relax a bit. We all chat about nothing in particular. Dad seems to tire very quickly and is in a deep sleep when we leave.

Here we are again around Dad's bed. A doctor comes in and says to Dad, "The antibiotics seem to have done the trick and you can go home today."

Fortunately the Macmillan nurse arrives just as he finishes speaking and says, "Mr Hughes is not going anywhere today. I need to make some arrangements before he can be discharged." She then gestures to me that I should go with her. Sitting in a side room, the nurse confirms she is in the process of securing Dad a place in a nursing home. Even though I know what she is doing, her words serve to open the floodgates and the tears flow freely with no attempt on my part to stop them. A tissue is thrust into my hand.

"I'm so sorry for you," she says, adding, "I know things are really difficult."

All I could think was, where is Dad going to go? I try to tell her through the snot and tears how important it is that he is in a place reasonably close to home. I don't know whether she realises that we all have limited sight and we rely upon taxis to get us about so it is essential that there are no lengthy journeys to unfamiliar places. Again, she says how sorry she is for us all and assures me she will do everything she can to find Dad a place near home. She confirms that Dad will remain where he is until after the Easter weekend and she will contact me on Tuesday with some news.

The Easter weekend seems interminable. We visit Dad every afternoon and evening. He is up and down over these few days, sometimes sitting up and chatting and all the time concerned about Mum, asking how she has been and hoping we are all getting enough sleep and looking after ourselves.

Easter Monday is Mum and Dad's wedding anniversary and Dad asks me to get a bouquet of flowers for Mum. He specifically asks me to tell her they are from him, but not to mention they are for their anniversary. I am a bit baffled at this latter instruction but I don't question his reason. I just do as he asks and present Mum with the lovely bouquet on Monday morning. I intend asking Dad why he does not want the anniversary mentioned but, with one thing and another, I do not get round to it. It doesn't really matter I suppose. Mum appears to love the flowers and I tell Dad when we visit him on Monday afternoon. Mum doesn't mention the flowers to Dad and I guess that she has forgotten all about them.

I receive a phone call from the Macmillan nurse on Tuesday morning confirming that a place is available for Dad at a nursing home, The Lime Trees, which is very close to Mum and Dad's home and they are expecting Dad tomorrow. She will make arrangements for an ambulance to transfer Dad from hospital to the nursing home and suggests that we might like to visit the home before then. The three of us visit the Lime Trees, which is only a short taxi journey away leaving Molly and Julie to look after Mum. We speak to the matron about Dad's care.

The place seems nice enough; it is a relatively new building and is bright and airy. Never having been in such a place before I don't know what to expect but the matron explains that all residents have their own room and the room reserved for Dad has an en suite with toilet and wash basin. We are shown around the communal dining area and lounge and we leave feeling that at least Dad is going to be really close to home and we will all be able to get there without too much difficulty. We are assured we can visit whenever and for as long as we wish.

And so on Wednesday 19 April, Dad is transferred from hospital into the care of the nursing home.

It isn't what I want for Dad. I had hoped he would spend his last days in his own home surrounded by those who loved him the most; although the nursing home was Dad's choice, I know for certain his motives are selfless. He has witnessed our distress and sadness over recent months and knows the toll Mum's illness is taking upon all three of us.

Many years later, this singular fact continues to bring a lump to my throat and the knowledge that their fifty-two year happy marriage had to end in such utter despair will haunt me forever.

9

FLOWERS AND VERSES.

It seems like an eternity since that grey November morning when we heard a nurse tell Dad he had cancer in his bowel, although the six months since then, when every moment of Dad's life became so precious and cherished, seem to have passed in the blink of an eye.

It is late April, a lovely spring day and the warmth in the air does nothing to lift the darkness and sorrow which threaten to overwhelm me.

There is much to be done. I cannot afford self-indulgence, Mum needs us to be strong and even though Mum's words and mood swings have been the cause of such anguish and despair, she now needs our strength and support more than ever.

Dad passed away at 1:00pm yesterday, 25 April, surrounded by 'his girls'. It was peaceful and I suppose if what is thus far, the most painful moment of my life could be described as lovely, then yes, it was lovely. I am certain Dad was aware of our presence even though he appeared barely conscious in the last hour. One of my nieces told us that when he opened his eyes, he was looking at my mum who was sitting close to his bed. At one point he moved his hand to touch hers. She seemed oblivious of the gesture and I hope with all my heart that Dad was unaware of her indifference at that moment.

We all sat with Dad for a while after he had passed away. I for one did not want to leave and I think the rest of my family felt the same. Following a chat with one of the medical staff to go over a few formalities, we returned to Mum's house where the rest of the day passed in a bit of a blur.

We had a number of visitors yesterday afternoon and evening – my mum's two sister's Iris and Dolly came to stay with Mum for a while and some of our cousins arrived last night. Mum does not seem to want people around the house; she appears to be in a world of her own and attempts to engage her in conversation are met with silence as if she does not hear us.

It's mid-morning. We have an appointment with the registrar and then we are going to the undertaker. Mum wants to use a long-established family firm who Mum and her siblings had used for both their parents, our grandparents.

"Do you want to get ready Mum? We will have to go soon."

"Where are we going?" she asks.

Eleanor sits beside her and takes her hand. "We have to go and register Dad's death and then go to the undertaker to arrange the funeral."

"Oh for goodness sake!" Mum exclaims. "There's no rush."

Her tone indicates she is not to be questioned further and my sisters and I sit quietly. I am wondering how best to approach Mum when I hear stifled weeping from across the room. It is Jane.

Eleanor asks, "Do you want a cup of tea Mum?"

"If I want a cup of tea I will make myself one!" she exclaims and her tone is hostile and serves to reduce Eleanor to tears. I am battling to stop the lump in my throat from exploding. I cannot speak and I sit with my head in my hands wondering, not for the first time, what we are going to do.

Presently, Mum goes to the phone muttering, "I'm going to phone our Iris." I hear her say, "These kids are telling me I have to go somewhere; I wish they would all sod off and leave me alone."

It breaks my heart to hear Mum's words. I honestly don't know whether she remembers that Dad has died and right now I am afraid to say anything to her.

Mum comes back into the lounge and sits down with no intention of getting ready to go out. She is still in her dressing gown and time is marching on. I don't know what the consequences will be if we miss the appointment with the registrar and I am starting to panic.

I go into the kitchen and put the kettle on. Eleanor joins me.

"What are we going to do?" she asks.

"I don't know," is all I can say.

I make a pot of tea. I have no idea why as nobody wants a cup, not even Mum which is extraordinary because she has never been known to refuse a cuppa, especially if there is a treat to go with it.

We are all in the lounge. It is quiet except for the intermittent sobs which the three of us are doing our best to stifle and suddenly it is like a shadow has lifted and a miraculous change occurs in Mum's demeanour. She gets to her feet and heads for the stairs.

"I better get dressed if we are going out," she exclaims and her tone tells us she is our mum again, not the stranger who has invaded her body so often recently.

"Do you want some help Mum?" Eleanor tentatively asks.

"Yes, come and sort my clothes out while I get washed."

Jane and I remain in the lounge and I exhale a long breath as the tension of the last few hours abates and my sadness for Dad comes crashing down around me.

Mum and Eleanor eventually come downstairs and we all get our coats and go to the registry office with Stewart who had arrived at the house when Mum was getting ready.

Thankfully, things go smoothly at the registrar's and relatively so at the funeral directors', although there are a few difficult moments when Mum appears not to know where she is, or for what reason. Sharon, who is taking instructions from Mum with some input from the three of us, seems to understand Mum's confusion and could not have been more helpful in guiding her through the options and decisions which had to be made.

We thank Sharon and leave, telling her we will return tomorrow when we will be able to see Dad. We make our way back to Mum's house and I am glad of Stewart's presence as he potters around making tea and something for us to eat. I think left to our own devices we would have just sat around doing nothing. All four of us are numb and exhausted following a truly harrowing twenty-four hours.

The next day the three of us, along with some of my nieces, go to the florist to order the floral tributes. Mum chooses not to come with us, instead she tells us what type of arrangement she wants so off we go and order the flowers from Mum, each of us and all of Dad's grandchildren and great grandchildren. We return to Mum's around lunchtime and we all manage a bite to eat before heading to the funeral parlour to see Dad.

The next day is spent finalising arrangements for the funeral. Notification of Dad's passing has to be phoned into the Liverpool Echo and this proves to be a particularly difficult and distressing task, as none of the four of us can see well enough to go through the verses We have to ask Jack to read us a selection of verses so we can each choose the one which means the most to us.

Jack, as usual, is happy to help and sets about reading out loud a selection of verses whilst the four of us sit in silence which is only broken by sniffles and stifled sobs from my sisters and I.

Mum is amazingly calm and composed as she interrupts Jack, stating, "I want the same verse as we used for Mam and Pop," and to our astonishment, she reeled off the verse word for word. Considering both her parents had passed away over forty years ago, Mum's recollection of the verse is amazing and takes us all by surprise.

I ask Mum whether she wants to go into Iris's house for a while. I feel that listening to Jack read out more verses for the three of us might be distressing for her. She stands up and says, "Good idea, I could do with a bit of fresh air."

As Iris only lives a few doors away, I suggest we go for a short walk before going. Mum agrees and I must confess the walk in the spring sunshine makes me feel a bit better and more able to deal with the sad task of selecting my dad's obituary.

As I return to Mum's house Eleanor and Jane have made their choices and Jack has written all three verses so he can phone them into the Echo. I make my choice and it becomes apparent how distressing this task has been for Jack. He had only lost his own dad months before and his own sadness is clear.

The rest of the day passes with family members popping in throughout the afternoon and evening and after everyone has left for the night, Mum goes to bed looking exhausted.

Eleanor and Jack return next morning. Jane says she will be up later and today we are going to organise the wake which will be held at Dad's beloved RNA club. As Dad was a former Royal Marine he is able to have a ceremonial flag held in salute as his funeral cortège passes by the club. Eleanor and Jack go to the RNA to make the arrangements with one of the officials.

Dad very rarely talked about his time in the Marines other than to reminisce about some of the places he had been. He particularly referred to both Cyprus and Malta being very beautiful islands and often thought he would like to revisit them, but he never spoke about the hostile environments and dangerous situations he had encountered.

I remember listening to Mum tell us about the time Dad was shipped out to Cyprus in January 1955, just a few days after the birth of Eleanor, Mum and Dad's first child. Having lived in Portsmouth prior to Eleanor's arrival and with Dad's imminent engagement overseas, Mum had returned to Liverpool to live with her Dad, "Pop". It was always a great source of amusement and pride when she recalled my Dad's return from this particular tour. Eleanor was eighteen months old by this time and, not knowing who this tall stranger in funny clothes was, used to run and hide behind her grandad's legs and refuse to look at Dad. Mum always used to laugh when she recalled this event and it became apparent that this was a particularly happy and proud time for my mum.

Mum's youngest sister, Reese, and her husband call to see us a couple of times in the days after Dad's death. Unfortunately, they will not be able to attend the funeral as they have a family holiday booked and as Auntie Reese is leaving the house she gives Mum a hug, telling her she will come and see her again as soon as she returns home after her holiday. Mum assures her youngest sister that she is OK adding, "As long as I've got my girls I will be fine."

I am a bit surprised at Mum's words as so often during Dad's illness, it felt like my sisters and I were the last people she wanted around.

Mum's youngest sister was the only sighted one of Mum's three remaining siblings and although she was not as consistent a feature in Mum's life as Iris and Dolly, she has become a more frequent visitor over recent years and regularly visited Mum since Dad's cancer diagnosis. Auntie Reese had unexpectedly arrived at the nursing home the day Dad passed away and her presence offered us some comfort.

For the first time in many months it seems like there is nothing to do and nothing to worry about. Yes, the sadness is almost unbearable but gone is the ever present dread of Mum's unpredictable and erratic behaviour being witnessed by Dad who was just too ill to bear it, and as awful as we all felt, there seems to be an implicit understanding that we can now focus on Mum's needs because, rightly or wrongly, I for one, had put my dad's needs before anything else and had not given Mum's illness as much consideration as I otherwise would have.

The rest of the day, when everyone has gone home and it is just me and Mum, is fairly uneventful. Mum is really quiet and now and again she says something about Dad and we chat about old times and some of the daft things my dad used to say which always made us chuckle. One of his favourite funnies was, when answering the door to a knock he would peep out of the window and if it was one of us three or any of his grandchildren, he would open the door just enough to be seen and tell the visitor in a sing-song voice, "not today thank you," and then go to close the door.

It is lovely to have my mum, my real mum, back with me. It may only be short-lived and even though it is a truly sad time, we talk a bit, I cry a lot as we drink gallons of tea. It is a joy to have this little bit of normality. Sad as we are, this is normal, grief is normal; the past months when Mum's illness had so cruelly taken her away from us and far worse, from Dad, who seemed to be so bewildered and saddened at Mum's deterioration, has been far from normal and was unbearable to witness.

Mum and I stay up later that night than we had for the longest time and when we eventually go to bed around 11:00pm Mum almost immediately falls into a deep sleep. I too fall asleep fairly quickly and for the first time in months, sleep soundly until morning.

As expected, Eleanor and Jane come back to Mum's house the next day. Some of their children popped in throughout the morning and we plan to go back to the funeral home later that day to see Dad.

Around lunchtime Dolly comes in to spend some time with Mum. She asks whether we can organise flowers from her, Iris and Reese. She goes on to ask whether we have put notifications in the Echo. Eleanor explains that we have already organised flowers and verses but will get somebody to help us do the same for them. I let out a long sigh, remembering how distressing both these tasks had been but accepting that Iris and Dolly, who, like my mum, are totally blind so can't manage to do these things themselves, it is perfectly normal that they would ask one of us to help them.

My frustration is not directed at Mum's sisters. I am a little bit peeved however that, just for once they might have turned to one of their many other nieces or nephews, all of whom are fully-sighted and live in very close proximity to my mum and her two sisters.

Looking back on things, I shouldn't have been surprised at my Auntie's request for help because this has been the way throughout our lives. Never once were any of our cousins asked for help, simply because they were never around. Both Iris and Dolly have been widowed for many years and both live alone. Despite this, they have had very little to no contact from their other nieces and nephews.

PART TWO

11

DATE AND TIME

It is four weeks since my dad passed away and I am heading to Mum's to spend a few days with her. None of us want Mum to be on her own for any length of time so my sisters visit every day, spending many hours with Mum and ensuring she has everything she needs and generally being there for company and offering comfort. My nieces and nephews, who all live close by, visit Mum regularly; Dolly often pops in to see her too.

Iris has always been the closest of Mum's siblings and she phones her several times each day to check that she is OK. Even though Iris lives just yards away she very rarely comes into Mum's house; the episode last summer when she hurt her foot seems to have had a profound affect upon her and she no longer wants to leave her home, even for the briefest time. Iris had spent three months 'incapacitated' last year following a minor accident at home when she sprained her foot.

Although we let Iris know about Mum's Alzheimer's diagnosis, she is reluctant to accept that Mum has any problem and insists that she is grieving, so her strange behaviour of late is only to be expected.

It was Iris who told Eleanor that Mum had phoned her just after Dad's funeral and said, "Will you phone me every morning and tell me what day it is?"

If ever a short sentence could rip my heart out, this was the one. I felt like I had been dealt a huge blow to my chest when Eleanor told me what Mum had asked of Iris.

Never before had I wished not to have heard something but you can't unknow what you know and this seemingly small insignificant bit of information sent me into a depth of sadness and grief; not only for the loss of my dad but the unimaginable emptiness left in my mum's life.

Growing up in a family with visual impairment, or as Mum would often refer to those of us who could not see properly, 'sight problems', had always been challenging, sometimes difficult and sometimes frustrating; but never did our predicament leave us sad or angry. We all just got on with whatever life threw at us with Mum being a formidable presence in our lives along with a determination and strength of character the likes of which I have never seen.

Yes, Dad was always there to pick up the slack when there were things which Mum's disability made it impossible for her to do herself, like reading the television page and dealing with the mail; otherwise there were very few things she couldn't manage.

When the three of us were young, Mum would take us to St Paul's Eye Hospital in Liverpool every year, usually around September, where we would spend most of the day undergoing various tests and invariably being paraded in front of a group of student doctors, as our eye condition is fairly rare.

There were often conflicting diagnoses for our condition depending upon which specialist we saw.

Sometime around the early Seventies, Mum took us to Moorfields Eye Hospital in London. The local specialist had arranged an appointment with Professor Laing at Moorfields who was interested in our family history.

Once again, and as expected, there was much discussion about us between the professor, other specialists and the obligatory contingent of student doctors.

It soon became apparent that there was some debate between the various specialists as to the exact condition which affected the majority of my family. It came as no surprise that Mum played a major part in the discussion. At one point she addressed Professor Laing asking, "How do you hope to help my family when you cannot even agree upon their condition?"

I cringed at Mum's words thinking oh my goodness Mum, you can't speak to a professor like that!

It was only later in life that I realised Mum was perfectly entitled to make her feelings known. By that time Mum and three of her siblings had lost all of their sight and it would only be a matter of time before the same fate would befall the three of us and two of our cousins.

I can remember with particular clarity Dad reading Mum's horoscope to her every Sunday afternoon. Mum used to say, "Read my fortune Dennis," and Dad would always respond, "You haven't got one," then continued with, "Gemini, let's see what Gemini is saying today," as he read the horoscope. Otherwise, if there was a way around obstacles that being blind threw at her, Mum would find it.

There was always a selection of equipment around, like talking scales and clocks as well as a device for audio books; the audio clocks and watches were scattered about the house so Mum always knew what time it was.

I shed buckets of tears upon learning of Mum's request to Iris. I really don't know why these few words had such an affect upon me. I only know that they did.

I try to pull myself together and put on my practical hat. I call the Royal National Institute for the Blind (RNIB) asking whether there is such a thing as a talking calendar. I have never heard of one but, as Mum would often say, "they can't shoot you for asking."

The lady I speak to could not have been more helpful. She is so patient as I try to explain through my tears what I need. She tells me they can supply a combined talking calendar/clock which I order to take to Mum on my upcoming visit.

I am relieved to see that the calendar/clock is a very simple device which I thought Mum would have no difficulty in using. It is a rectangular shape, about the size of a small house brick, with two prominent buttons on top with all the gubbins securely tucked away inside a cover on the underside, which is pretty difficult to remove.

The design of it is extremely beneficial as one particular aspect of Mum's behaviour is her constant fiddling with anything and everything that is not nailed down, which inevitably results in whatever she interferes with being taken to pieces and in some cases rendered completely useless. The remote control for the television is forever being taken apart and the batteries lost and Mum would phone Jane regularly to say the television was broken. Poor Jane, she bore the brunt of Mum's mishaps in those early days simply because she lived closest to Mum and would always come running whenever Mum needed help. Sometimes Jane would arrive home after spending several hours with Mum, only to be greeted by her ringing phone. It would be Mum complaining that she couldn't find this or that, so Jane would turn around and go straight back round, often to find the lost item sitting on the mantelpiece or fallen down beside the armchair.

I arrive at Mum's early afternoon. Eleanor and Jane are both there and I proudly show off the new device and hand it to Mum who doesn't seem too impressed. Nevertheless she sits playing with the buttons constantly. That's good, I think, she has got the hang of it. The first hour or so of that visit consists of us enjoying tea and cake and listening to the automated voice tell us over and over, "It's Tuesday 23 May 2006, it's 2:36pm," and so on and so on.

I nudge Eleanor saying, "The battery will go before the end of today!"

We have a bit of a giggle. I think we are all just relieved to see Mum getting to grips with her new aid.

The next morning Mum gets up early as she usually does. At this time she is still mobile and able to find her way around the house safely and perform most simple tasks. As she so often has done in the past, she brings a cup of tea into my room asking whether I want something to eat. I sigh as I check my own watch which tells me it is 6:15am. I thank Mum for my cuppa and say I will get up in a little while. I hear her pottering around downstairs. The radio has been switched on and I hear activity in the kitchen which tells me she is making herself some breakfast.

I go downstairs and am dismayed to find the talking clock in pieces on the mantelpiece.

"What happened to your new clock?" I ask.

"What new clock?" she asks.

"Remember the talking clock I gave you yesterday, the one which tells you what day it is."

"Oh it broke and I tried to fix it," is her immediate response.

The bottom cover is nowhere to be seen and one of the two batteries is beside the clock and the other one is on the floor. I exhale as I think, bloody hell, how did she manage this? The bottom cover is fairly robust and very securely attached requiring a small screwdriver to remove it so I am baffled as to how she has managed to take it apart. I eventually find all the pieces and reset the date and time before putting the clock back together. I find a couple of double-sided sticky tabs and stick the clock to the mantelpiece, telling Mum to leave it there so she will always know where it is and it will be easier to use if it is stuck down.

Later that day I take Mum to Iris's house for a while. I had phoned Iris to ask whether she would like to come in and spend some time with Mum, but she declined saying, "No, bring your mum here instead." It is a fairly uneventful day. We have dinner around 6:00pm, watch a bit of television and have an early night.

Mum is never one for staying up late, preferring to go to bed and listen to her talking books. As usual she is up very early the next morning and after breakfast I go to the local shop; upon my return I am dismayed to see the talking clock in pieces once again. As before the gubbins are scattered around and I put it back together again, resetting the date and time.

Eleanor is coming to see us later on so I ask her to bring some parcel tape from the hardware store at the end of her road.

I wrap the tape around the entire surface of the clock, leaving only the two prominent buttons at the top exposed; it looks a right sight but at least it will be virtually impossible for Mum to take apart.

Hmmm, who was I kidding! The clock did remain intact for the duration of my visit, mainly because every time she used it I would encourage her to leave it where it was! However the day after I returned home, Jane phoned to say the clock was once again in bits, this time with strands of the sticky tape tangled around it.

"We will just have to keep on fixing it" I tell Jane. "Hopefully she will lose interest and find something less significant to destroy."

This proves to be the case as over the coming months and years various things around the house either disappear for long periods, only to be found later in the most unlikely place, or many items are either damaged or even destroyed with Mum insisting, "I don't know how that happened!"

The smallest bedroom has a sliding door in order to maximise the floorspace and on one occasion the door had been completely removed from the track along the bottom, leaving it hanging precariously on the hanger at the top. It did not matter how many times the door was fixed, next time Mum was left alone the door would 'mysteriously' come off its runners.

Eventually we had the door taken off, worried that it might only be a matter of time before she hurt herself as a result of her fiddling.

I telephone Mum every day when I am in my own home. Although I am two hundred miles away, she is never far from my thoughts. Sometimes days and even weeks can go by with her displaying no particularly disturbing signs of any problems, other than the constant repetition, which has become a regular and expected feature of any conversation and of course the forgetfulness.

On one occasion Stewart accompanies me on a five day visit to Mum's. After dinner on the last night we are standing side by side at the sink, washing up after dinner. Mum remains at the table with a cup of tea when she asks, "When are we having our dinner?"

Stewart turns to me and sighs.

"We have just eaten Mum," I say. "Remember, it was one of your favourites: sausage and mash with onion gravy."

After no more than a few seconds, the question comes again.

"We have had dinner already Mum," I say, and carry on with the washing up.

Once again, "What are we having for dinner?"

This time Stewart turns to me. He's only inches from my face and I sense his frustration as he lets out a long sigh and exclaims, "Can't you do something about that?"

A bit weary and frustrated myself, I was about to react badly and hurl my own pent-up frustration with Mum in Stewart's direction, however just in time I realise the futility of this and instead turn to my husband and say, **"WELCOME TO ALZHEIMER LAND."**

We finish the dishes and I join Mum at the table while Stewart watches television in the lounge.

Mum seems to be coping really well, living independently with only minimal input from the Cherry Tree who have arranged for a CPN to visit mum periodically and a carer calls in every morning to ensure she regularly takes her medication.

Mum has always enjoyed good health; the only long term medication she required up until now was iron tablets and thyroxine for an underactive thyroid. In June 2006 she is prescribed Aricept by her consultant psychiatrist. We were told that, although Alzheimer's is incurable, the Aricept may help to manage the symptoms of mild to moderate Alzheimer's. Ordinarily the Aricept is given at bedtime and it is important that the single tablet which Mum was prescribed is taken at the same time every day. The consultant agreed that it would be OK if Mum is given her tablet in the morning by the care worker, thereby ensuring the tablets are correctly administered.

I am back at Mum's just before the Aricept is provided as she needs to undergo an Electrocardiogram (ECG) as the medication may not be suitable if there are any problems with her heart. Mum is given the OK and the single tablet to be taken once a day is duly prescribed.

Mum wants to know why she needed the ECG. I tell her that Mr Addlington from the Cherry Tree, had arranged the test. She seems to accept this without further question. The first time Mr Addlington came to see Mum was when Dad was still alive. Mum found a box of chocolates on the kitchen table shortly after his visit, they had been brought by Jack later that same day but Mum always insisted, "That nice Mr Addlington brought me some chocolates."

We did not realise it at the time but this little misunderstanding turned out to be a bit of a blessing, as whenever the CPN came to visit Mum, we only had to mention that the visitor had been sent by Mr Addlington, to ease her anxiety.

I remain at Mum's for the first week following the introduction of the Aricept. Although there are a myriad of side effects which may be experienced, Mum shows no signs of any, which is a huge relief. We decide that one of us will stay with Mum day and night for the first couple of weeks following the introduction of the medication, just in case.

12

DOING REALLY WELL

I remember one particular visit to Mr Addlington's clinic. It was around nine or ten months after Mum's diagnosis, and was just a routine visit which, in the event, Mum attended regularly twice a year over the next five years. On this particular visit Mr Addlington surprised us by stating, "I fully expected your mum to be in full-time residential care by now."

Well, what can I say, I have already mentioned Mum's strength of character and I think Mr Addlington was beginning to realise that she was not just your average Alzheimer's patient; she was something pretty special. Having said that, the more I learn about this wretched disease, the more I realise there is probably no such thing as 'average' when it comes to the manifestation of symptoms.

Mum, God bless her, would never question these sessions at the Cherry Tree, she just sat listening and occasionally told Mr Addlington she was "not so bad thanks" when he asked her how she was.

These sessions would usually start with a chat whilst Mum was present and then one of us would take her to sit in the waiting room whilst the two remaining would fill the consultant in on any significant changes in Mum's behaviour.

We would usually leave after being told, "Your mum is doing really well and I will see her again in six months."

Weeks turned into months and Christmas that first year after we had lost Dad is particularly sad, not only because it is the first Christmas without him, but the memory of the awful events of last Christmas are never far from our minds.

I travel to Mum's on Christmas Eve. Stewart and I, along with Mum, are to have dinner the following day with Eleanor and her family. Jane will have her family dinner at her own home, and on Christmas morning we visit Jane armed with presents for her family.

Jane cannot contain her emotions as she unwraps her gift.

My dad had been presented with a certificate for crossing the Arctic Circle in November 1952 when he was in the Royal Marines. I recall my mum telling us that Dad's ship, HMS Vanguard, went there on manoeuvres to test cold climate clothing for the Military.

The certificate has a large Neptune down the entire length on the left with the greeting from the King of the Sea inscribed down the right hand side. Although the document is a bit fragile it is in pristine condition considering it is more than fifty years old.

I had the certificate mounted and framed as a gift for Jane and as she unwraps it on Christmas morning, even though, by this time, Jane has lost most of her sight, as soon as I explain what is in the large picture frame, her delight and sadness are evident in equal measure.

I had thought long and hard about giving the certificate to Jane; after all it now belonged to my mum. However, over recent months she had gone on a clearing-out spree around the house, disposing of anything and everything regardless of it's worth. Cutlery and crockery were the first casualties of these clearing-out episodes; it seemed like each time I visited, there were fewer belongings in the cupboards and drawers. I was concerned that it might only be a matter of time before she did the same with more important items so I decided to remove those things which were irreplaceable, and keep them safely at my own home. I didn't feel good about this but thought it necessary to safeguard important documents.

We get through Christmas that year with more than a few tears and lots of laughter, which always accompanies our family get-togethers, and when I eventually return to my own home on New Year's Eve I am relieved that the holiday period is over.

13

LADIES' DAY

What a difference a year makes!

I am up early; Mum and I are in the kitchen in our dressing gowns eating breakfast. We are looking forward to the day ahead.

I don't remember feeling this excited for the longest time and Mum seems to be looking forward to the day too.

Yes, Dad is dead and Mum has Alzheimer's – both these facts sadden and frustrate me but when I remember this same weekend last year, when I thought I would never smile again, well, what can I say; there is no comparison.

Mum seems to be doing reasonably well, taking everything into account. She remains in her own home living semi-independently with family visiting every day and a hot meal delivered daily, courtesy of Meals on Wheels. She is still able to make her breakfast and snacks and manages small tasks around the house although it is noticeable that some particular tasks, like changing the bed, are beginning to elude her. We find ways around things as and when they occur; no point in worrying or fretting too much about the gradual decline. We just deal with things as they happen. The issue of the bedding is particularly distressing and it takes several months to find a way around it because whenever one of us attempts to strip the bed, Mum will come upstairs demanding to know what we think we are doing. She usually becomes irate and hurls abuse insisting that she had "changed the bloody bed yesterday so get the hell out of my house!"

On one such occasion, Mum catches me halfway through changing the bed and as usual she rants that the bed was only just changed.

"Oh Mum," I say gently. "I wish you had told me before, I could have saved myself a job." Miraculously, Mum's anger dissolves as she says, "Shall I help?"

It is early April and the Grand National will be run tomorrow; as is usual for the world famous steeplechase, the day before the main event is Ladies Day, an opportunity for us girls to dress up in all our finery, have a nice meal and if so inclined, a flutter or two on the races. Of course we will, we are not our dad's daughters for nothing!

This weekend last year was the time of 'the bucket, the bed and the heart attack' which turned out to be Dad's last weekend at home.

I help mum get dressed in a lovely three piece cream suit bought especially for the occasion. Her lovely silver hair has been beautifully styled and the outfit is topped with a fedora-type hat in a dark bronze shade. She looks stunning and I am so proud and delighted that we are all going to have what promises to be a day to remember. Our tickets include a meal in one of the hospitality venues as well as access to the main stand close to the finish line. The forecast is for a warm dry day; it's all looking good for a lovely day together.

Julie and Jane will be here shortly, then I will call a cab to take us to the racecourse which is only a couple of miles away. We will meet Eleanor, Molly and Jade there.

The day turns out to be as brilliant as we had hoped with Mum tucking into her meal with obvious relish and then insisting that she will come to the stand, which involves a trek up three flights of stairs. I had thought she would prefer to remain in the comfort of the hospitality marquee and suggest that we can take turns at staying with her but no, she is determined to be in on the action, so we all stand leaning against the rail as the horses thunder past. Some of us have a flutter so there is a lot of screaming and shouting encouragement; it seems like the perfect opportunity to really rid ourselves of the sadness and despair which has enveloped our family over the past eighteen months. For a short while at least, we are a normal happy family enjoying a day out.

I remain at Mum's house for a few more days, and decide to give the place a bit of a spring clean. I tell Mum I will clean the windows while she is listening to the radio. To my surprise and delight Mum says, "I can do that, you do something else."

I hand Mum the bottle of Windowlene and a cloth and off she trots towards the patio doors and proceeds to spray the glass, then rub vigorously. I remember just standing there, watching and smiling. It was lovely to see her as the Mum she had always been. Capable and enthusiastic in whatever she did.

Although Mum has not worked in many years, she had many skills which made her a wonderful home-maker. Often we would come home from school to the lovely aroma of scones or pastries baking in the oven. She was a great cook and always managed to produce something scrumptious for dinner.

Sometimes she had small burn marks on her arms where she had caught it on a hot tray whilst taking something from the oven. This always saddened me as it was a very rare occurrence whereby Mum's blindness would be an issue. She never complained and more often than not, when asked what had happened to her arm would say, "I don't know, what is wrong with it?" That was as much as she would say about the mishap.

When we were younger and all still living at home, Dad and the three of us would either go to work or school whilst Mum would remain at home with her chores, listening to the radio and preparing for her family to return. It was always obvious when the windows had been cleaned as, upon my return, before I even took my coat off, I would go around the house straightening the lace curtains which had been disturbed as Mum cleaned the windows. Other indications of Mum's industry was evident by pictures being skew-whiff and ornaments out of alignment.

In 1979 Mum applied to be considered for a guide dog. She was duly assessed and considered suitable to undergo the relevant training. Following a month at the guide dog training centre in Bolton, Vanya, a gorgeous German Shepherd which was the colour of a yellow Labrador, became Mum's constant companion.

It took a bit of getting used to; Mum would take herself off to the local shops or to Eleanor's house which was close-by at that time. Vanya certainly gave her a whole new lease of life and she made the most of her new-found independence. It was a joy to see and the addition of Vanya into our family proved to be an absolute blessing for all of us.

Mum ended up having three guide dogs throughout her life.

14

IF YOU ARE THERE, YOU ARE THERE

It's the last Friday in the month around mid-morning and Mum and I are waiting for the minibus that will take us to the Alzheimer's support group which Mum attends each month. Usually one of my sisters accompanies her but I have been staying with her this past week so I am taking her today.

Beside us on the bus is an elderly couple. Well, I say elderly, they are probably around Mum's age, maybe even a bit younger but until now I haven't ever thought of Mum in that way.

It soon becomes apparent that it is the wife who is caring for her husband. He is quiet and unresponsive to any of her questions or prompts. I engage in conversation with her explaining that Mum is in the early stages of Alzheimer's and following the death of our dad the previous year we are still on a learning curve whilst trying to give her as much support and normality as possible.

The wife (I am ashamed to admit I didn't catch her name) tells me that her husband is in a fairly advanced stage of Alzheimer's and whilst she is his main carer, she does have someone come in to sit with him two evenings each week so that she can switch off and get a decent night's sleep.

I remember thinking in my ignorance, that I didn't see the point in that. I mean, if you are there you are there; I could not understand the benefit of having someone else in your home at the same time.

My goodness, little did I realise how wrong I was in my thinking! I would soon come to understand how unbelievably, unimaginably, wonderful such help would prove to be.

We pile into the hall where we are greeted by a couple of the organisers and I tell them I am Annie's middle daughter and I live in Scotland, which is why I haven't been here before. I am made welcome and we are directed to a table where a few others are already seated. The couple from the bus sit beside us. Once more the husband is quiet; his wife undoes his jacket and helps him take it off. She tells him he is about to have his lunch as a plate of sandwiches is placed in front of him by a helper. It is at that moment I think for the first time, gosh, it is like having a small child in an adult's body, and feel so grateful that Mum's condition is not too bad in comparison.

Mum is fairly animated, asking why we are here and exclaiming how hungry she is.

"It's OK," I tell her, "there are some lovely sandwiches and sausage rolls here and we are getting a cup of tea in a minute."

"Oh good," she says. "Are we going home after that?"

This was a relatively new feature of Mum's behaviour; whenever she went out, even if it was just into Iris's house, she would immediately ask when she would be going home. Likewise, when at home, she was asking more and more, "Are we going out today?"

I explain we are here for lunch and a bit of a natter, then we will be going home. She seems content as she tucks into her lunch and responds, "well I suppose it saves on the washing up."

Mum often made that comment whenever she was taken out for a meal, when asked whether she enjoyed whatever she had eaten she would always finish with "It saves on the washing up."

We are back at Mum's house and I call Jane to let her know how the afternoon went. I tell her about the couple on the bus and say how lucky we are that Mum is nothing like as bad as that poor man.

I remember thinking in my ignorance that being a bit forgetful and repetitious at times was not the end of the world and whilst Mum's behaviour could be frustrating, even maddening at times, it was not too terrible when compared to what I saw today. It's amazing how easy it is to convince yourself that things are, or will be, a certain way when the alternative is too awful to contemplate.

I would later come to realise that, either consciously or unconsciously, I had suspended any thoughts about the future and the impact Mum's illness would have upon her and consequently us as a family.

Over the coming months there are some changes in Mum's condition, some fairly innocuous with no cause for alarm. One distressing aspect was the increasing lack of personal hygiene. When challenged she would insist, "I had a bath yesterday," or, "My hair does not need washed, I did it this morning," when it was obvious that neither was true. It is sad to see her appearance decline in this way and impossible to know what to do for the best. This was one area whereby when challenged she would become unbelievably aggressive, bordering upon violent.

We raise the problem with Mum's CPN who comes to have a chat with her and leaves, telling us, "you are doing a good job, just carry on as you are."

Not really much help and we decided to leave things be for the time being; hoping that she would soon get over this particular phase.

Other things however, cannot be ignored. The most significant being an incident with the gas which led to the cooker having to be disconnected.

Whilst recounting this episode which I found especially sad and still upsets me to this day, I am reminded of another incident in the early days of Mum's illness which I have to admit makes me cringe with embarrassment but has my sisters howling with laughter.

It's Saturday evening. Mum seems settled in her armchair with a cup of tea and a gooey cream cake which makes a terrible mess whilst she tucks in. What the heck, I tell myself, I'll clean it up later. I finish my own goody and ask Mum whether she enjoyed her cake. As usual she responds, "Oooh yes, it's lovely."

We settle down to watch an old episode of Inspector Morse on ITV3 and as I relax after another eventful day with lots of visitors and a trip to the local shop with Mum, I keep getting a faint whiff of gas which disappears so quickly that I think I must be imagining things.

Around 10:00pm we decide to go to bed so I help Mum upstairs after closing the kitchen window and locking the doors.

Before going upstairs I have a quick sniff around the kitchen; the smell of gas earlier was bothering me but in that moment it is not noticeable.

Mum is safely tucked up in bed, so I decide to go back downstairs for one last check in the kitchen.

This time there is no mistake. A smell hits me, not especially strong but nevertheless most definitely there.

I quickly open the window which I had closed minutes before and go back upstairs into Mum's room telling her, "Mum, we have to go into Iris's house, I think there is a gas leak somewhere."

I am relieved when she does not question my words but gets out of bed and takes her dressing gown and slippers from me. I quickly telephone Iris to let her know we are on our way in; she has the door open as we walked up her path.

I phone gas emergency to be told somebody will be out within the hour.

Sure enough, the Transco van arrives about twenty minutes later and I accompany the gas engineer into Mum's house whilst she remains with her sister.

The gas engineer agrees that there is a faint smell of something. He uses a device to check the meter which is tucked away in a cupboard at one end of the kitchen. Then the boiler, cooker and gas fire get the same treatment.

To my surprise, and relief, he confirms that he has found no indication of problems with any of the appliances. He seems a bit baffled and eventually asks if there is something rotten in the bin or perhaps the fridge.

With as much indignation as I can muster, I open the sink unit door which contains the waste bin followed by the fridge. How dare you suggest there is something rotten in Mum's kitchen, I think.

He tells me he needs to go to his van for another instrument and in the few moments it takes a lightbulb moment hits me.

"Oh no, oh bloody hell no!' I curse myself but can't help giggling.

I open the oven door and am immediately hit by the whiff of Mum's three day old Meals on Wheels container which she had tucked away and then forgotten about.

I am mortified and too embarrassed to tell the gas engineer when he returns.

My stupidity is compounded by not confessing my mistake as the engineer tells me, "there does not seem to be a problem but just in case, I will have to condemn the boiler until it is properly checked out in the morning."

I eventually bring Mum home and when I tell Iris what has happened she tries to give me a lecture for causing such a fuss but I know she is also trying to contain her own amusement.

15

PUT THE KETTLE ON

A far more worrying and potentially dangerous development involving the gas presented itself some months later.

I am back in my own home and have just enjoyed dinner and a glass of wine. "I'll just give Mum a call before it gets much later," I tell Stewart.

The phone rings for the longest time but that's alright, Mum moves about slowly and it's not unusual for Mum not to pick up right away.

"Hello," she sounds harassed and a bit flustered, "Hi Mum, it's Liz, how are you?"

"Oh not so bad," comes her usual response.

We chat about her day. She struggles to tell me who has been to visit her. I already know of course as one or both of my sisters visit every day, as do some of my nieces.

We have been particularly worried over recent weeks as on three separate occasions Mum has left the gas on in the oven – the first two occasions either myself or one of my sisters was in the house at the time so there was no real harm done but the last time it happened gave us all a real fright and we realise we have to take action to keep her safe.

On the day in question, Eleanor arrives at Mum's house around 10:00am. As soon as Mum opens the door a strong smell of gas hits Eleanor and she rushes inside telling Mum to stay at the front door. Eleanor said the gas was so strong she feared turning on the light in the kitchen in case the whole house went up with a bang.

She quickly turns off the cooker and opens the back door and windows. By this time Mum has made her way back into the lounge and is sitting in her chair, oblivious to Eleanor's frantic action.

Upon learning of this episode I travel to Mum's house and decide to stay for a few days as we realise that steps need to be taken in order to keep her safe in her own home. We decide the only thing to do is to have the oven disconnected and tell Mum it is broken. We know we will have to think long and hard about how best to manage this new phase that Mum seems to have slipped into. Up until recently she has been coping really well living on her own with the family visiting her every day. Yes, she is becoming increasingly forgetful and sometimes seems more confused than usual, however the episodes with the gas cannot be ignored.

As Mum uses a kettle on the hob I purchase a new electric one with the intention of getting her used to it during the time I am with her.

I purposefully keep telling Mum, "I would love a cup of tea Mum, would you make me one?" She is always happy to oblige and soon becomes familiar with using the new kettle and after a week I return home confident that Mum is still able to make herself a hot drink. Anyway, this particular night when I phone she slips into the conversation that the kettle does not work so she has made her cup of tea in the microwave. I doubted that the recently purchased kettle was broken and after a bit of persuasion, Mum admits that she does not know how it works.

I can't express how much her words sadden me; she does not appear too concerned about this and is quite matter-of-fact when telling me about her difficulty in using the kettle.

As happens so often lately, I become tearful and Stewart sighs in exasperation asking, "What's wrong now?" I explain what Mum has told me and become more and more distressed at this small but significant deterioration in her condition.

Stewart becomes increasingly annoyed. I know it is only because he hates to see me upset, but his mood only serves to compound my distress as I tell him, "She doesn't know how to use the kettle."

"Oh for God's sake!" he exclaimed. "Phone one of your nieces and tell them to go and make her a cup of tea." He appears to have missed the point entirely and is genuinely dumfounded at my distress.

16

EXTRA HELP

Jane has been doing battle with Social Services to try and get some additional help to enable us to keep Mum in her own home. We have decided between us that someone needs to be with her day and night since the incident with the gas and the realisation that Mum can no longer make a phone call without help.

Following months of phone calls, meetings and correspondence with Social Services, Mum is awarded an allowance which enables us to employ a carer to stay with her three nights per week. This proves to be an absolute godsend particularly as Jane's daughter Molly, who is spending a lot of time with Mum, volunteers to give up her own employment in order to become Mum's carer for a significant period. This allows the three of us to divide our time looking after Mum in a more structured way; we produce a rota which allows us to plan our own lives around the time spent caring for her.

This arrangement works well for many months and even though Mum's condition is deteriorating quite noticeably, at least we know she is safe and has company twenty-four hours a day (with the exception of one hour on Saturday and Sunday evenings) although, before too long it becomes apparent that even this small window will have to be closed.

17

FINISH THE CALL

It is now getting on for five years since Mum's diagnosis. It's mid-November 2010 and is exactly the kind of day which makes November my least favourite month. It has been the dullest of days with hardly any light in the sky. It's not especially cold, just damp and drizzly; the lack of daylight always manages to leave me feeling a bit down and longing for springtime when days are so much brighter and longer.

I have been busy in the kitchen today doing the one thing which makes days like this less miserable, making batches of soup for the freezer.

It is Saturday and one of only two days each week when Mum is on her own for a brief period; there is a one hour gap between 6:00-7:00pm when the afternoon carer leaves and the night sitter arrives. Mum is still mobile and able to find her way around, doing little things for herself.

I phoned mum just after 6:00pm; it is not an easy thing to do, maintaining a conversation when she has almost no short-term memory.

I start with my usual greeting.

"Hi Mum, it's Liz from bonny Scotland."

I use this term as I think it helps Mum recognise which of her three daughters she is speaking to.

I ask how she is.

"Oh not so bad," comes the expected response.

"Have you had any visitors today?" I ask.

"Hmmm," she ponders. "No I don't think anyone was here today."

This never ceases to sadden me as I know that as well as her carers, both my sisters have been at Mum's house today. I try to prompt her into remembering by asking, "Did Jane come to see you today?"

A brief silence and then she replies, "No, nobody has been today."

My sadness is compounded as I realise the loneliness which must exist in her mind. "Oh well Mum," I try to lighten my tone as I tell her, "Julie will be coming to see you soon; she will be staying at your house tonight so you will have company."

"When will she be here?" she asks.

"Probably in about half an hour."

"Oh that's good, will she be staying for a while?"

"Yes Mum, she is going to stay with you all night."

"When will she be coming?"

"Soon Mum, she will be there soon," I say.

We chat like this for a while longer then I tell Mum that I have to go, my dinner is on the table and I remind her that Julie will be there soon.

I wait, as I always do, until I hear Mum replace the receiver. I don't know when I started this habit, nor do I fully understand why I do it. I think it gives me a little bit of reassurance that all is well, as though the act of replacing the receiver signals that she is in control and able to perform simple tasks. This is nonsense of course, but it's amazing how you can persuade yourself that things are OK when the reality is a million miles away.

I hear Mum mumbling to herself, "Right, where does this go; oh no that's not it. I think that's a coat."

I realise that she has wandered across the hall and is trying to find the phone so she can replace the handset. I try to attract her attention by shouting down the phone so that we can just carry on chatting until Julie arrives but Mum is oblivious to my shouts; she continues feeling her way around the hall mumbling to herself.

My throat feels ready to burst as I try to hold back the tears. I feel utterly helpless as Mum continues to struggle. Eventually the phone goes quiet and I hear Mum's footsteps move away. I learn later that the receiver had been discarded on the stair.

I immediately call Eleanor and I try not to sound too distressed but the minute I speak she knows something is wrong. I burst into tears as I explain what has just happened. She too becomes upset telling me that she thought Mum seemed a bit more confused than usual when she visited earlier. She said she would find out how long Julie would be, so we finish the call and she promises to phone me right back.

Ten minutes later Eleanor is in a taxi on her way to Mum's. She has not been able to get hold of Julie, however, upon her arrival at Mum's house, she is greeted by Julie who had arrived a few minutes earlier. Mum is fine and Eleanor stays for a while before returning to her own home. We are comforted in the knowledge that

Mum is no longer alone and are determined that from now on she would not be left on her own , even for the briefest period.

18

CLEARING OUT

Many aspects of our lives have changed as we continue to cater for Mum's needs.

A lot of the aggression, which upon reflection, was one of the most distressing and difficult aspects of her behaviour, has disappeared. Indeed, these days she is compliant and amiable to anything requested of her. Mercifully, the personal hygiene issue is no longer a problem. She is bathed every morning without complaint, which we consider a huge victory and a lesson in patience and perseverance.

All three of us are with Mum today as she has a hospital appointment which we all want to attend.

We are in the lounge and for once, there is no tea and cake to enjoy.

"I think I need to go to the toilet."

Mum is sitting in her usual armchair and the three of us are close by. At her words we all spring into action. Eleanor takes Mum's hand and says, "Come on Mum, up you get, quick as you can."

Eleanor helps her upstairs, trying to move quickly whilst causing her as little alarm as possible.

"I think I've got the runs," Mum says when she and Eleanor are near the top of the stairs.

"Oh no, please not again!" I exclaim as I follow them upstairs.

Eleanor eventually gets Mum to the bathroom and manoeuvres her onto the toilet.

Too late! The mess is on the bathroom floor and Mum has to be stripped from the waist down. Slippers, bath mat and Mum's clothes all go into a poly bag to be sorted later. Eleanor is trying to comfort Mum, assuring her that everything is OK and we will get her cleaned up in no time. Mum vomits without warning and I attend to her whilst Eleanor runs downstairs to find a bowl. Eleanor slips in her haste to get downstairs, the phone rings and Jane answers. I hear her tell the caller, "Well she is fine but Eleanor has slipped and I have to help her; I'll call you back in a minute."

Jane puts the phone down and comes to help Eleanor who is not too badly hurt, just a bit shaken and overwhelmed by today's events.

Jane helps Eleanor to a chair and then finds a bowl which she brings up to me in case Mum is sick again.

The vomiting is mercifully short-lived and I ask Jane to run the bath so that we can get Mum cleaned up properly.

It's truly awful seeing her in such a state and her distress is hard to bear but right now I have to close my mind to my disquiet and get on with making sure she is OK.

Mum hasn't complained once about what she is going through today.

Jane and I are washing Mum in the bath while Eleanor gets a new set of clothes ready for her. Between the three of us we get her dried and dressed and we all go downstairs and try to relax for a while.

Mum seems none the worse for her ordeal.

Jane calls Iris to let her know what has happened and reassures her that Mum is fine and Eleanor is no worse off after her fall. Iris constantly worries about Mum and is becoming increasingly concerned about the three of us, asking on a regular basis how we are coping. .

It was Iris who had called in the midst of the mayhem and I knew she would be concerned, not only about Mum but hearing about Eleanor's fall. This too would be preying on her mind. Jane asks Iris whether she would like to come and sit with us but as she so often did, Iris declines stating, "No, it sounds like you three have got enough on your plate looking after your Mum, just let me know how things are when you get back from the hospital."

Just over a week ago one of the carers who had been looking after Mum expressed concerns after helping her on the toilet, spotted what looked like blood in her stools. We immediately contacted the GP who arranged for a colonoscopy to be done as soon as possible

Today is the preparation for the procedure; the 'clearing out' process. Having witnessed this with my dad before his bowel cancer diagnosis, the distress to Mum, coupled with the worry about the outcome of the test, was really worrying for us all.

The procedure is scheduled for 3:00pm and all four of us take a taxi to the hospital around 2:30pm. We approach the reception at the clinic and are advised things are running a bit behind schedule but we should take a seat in the waiting room.

I am horrified to see how crowded the waiting room is.

After a short while a nurse comes in and announces that clinic is running about ninety minutes late so if anyone does not want to wait they should make themselves known at reception and an appointment can be made for another day.

The distress and trauma that Mum has experienced over the past twenty-four hours to enable this procedure to be carried out is not something we want to put her through again so we decide to wait it out and hope things will not be too much longer.

One or two patients decide to make alternative appointments and I hope their departure will speed things up. Mum is becoming a bit agitated asking why she is here and when will it be her turn.

A further hour passes and I go to find somebody who can tell me how much longer we are likely to be waiting. I explain about Mum's condition and how she is confused and agitated. The nurse assures me that Mum is next on the list but this doesn't really answer my question.

After a further fifteen minutes Mum is called and I stand up to accompany her out of the waiting room. The nurse is less than friendly and tells me, "You cannot come with her," and starts to walk on ahead. I follow her and almost have to beg her to listen to me before I relinquish Mum into her care.

"My mum is blind," I tell her, "she cannot be left to her own devices."

"You cannot come any further," she tells me as though I had not spoken.

"Excuse me," I insist, "My mum is blind; she also has Alzheimer's and doesn't fully understand what is going on."

I repeat that Mum cannot be left alone, the nurse softens a little and takes Mum's arm assuring me that she will be well looked after.

I return to the waiting room where my two sisters are sitting and we decide to make our way to the cafeteria for a cuppa whilst we wait for Mum.

It is only because we are all very familiar with this hospital that we are able to find our way to the coffee shop. We are helped to find somewhere to sit and a customer, having witnessed our struggle, very kindly comes to the counter with me and helps carry our tea back to the table.

We eventually make our way back to where we left Mum. We have been told she will be taken to the recovery ward following her procedure. We have no idea where this is, but suppose it will be fairly close by. We arrive back at the reception area and ask to be directed.

"It's just along the corridor and when you get to the double doors you should turn left, it is right there, you can't miss it," we are advised by the receptionist. She then notices that all three of us are using white canes and apologises unnecessarily for her words. She comes out of her office and reiterates her directions, emphasising the route in an attempt to make things easier for us.

We thank her and say we should be OK.

"I'll watch you until you get to the end of the corridor," she says and we thank her again as we start to move.

A nurse comes toward us and tells us, "You cannot come along here, there are theatres up here, where are you going?"

Eleanor explains that we need to get to the recovery ward and have been pointed in this direction.

She repeats, "You cannot come this way; if you go back the way you came, then go down to the ground floor and through the day clinics until you come to a flight of stairs which will bring you to the other side of this corridor, someone will be able to direct you from there." She hurries away before any of us can protest.

"For Christ sake!" Eleanor proclaims, "Nothing is easy is it? She could see how we are fixed, I'm sure we could have just cut through."

"Let's go," I say. "Are you ok Jane? Hold onto my arm."

Jane has the least sight of the three of us and it is always a bit daunting making our way around, especially when there are stairs to negotiate.

We eventually reach the recovery ward and are directed into another room where the nurse explains that the test had proved to be inconclusive and they will have to do the procedure again in a couple of weeks. I think by this time all three of us were so overwhelmed by the events of the day that the longest moment passed without a word from any of us. Jane was the first one to speak, exclaiming, "What do you mean, inconclusive, did the test reveal any problem? Why does it have to be done again?"

I am dismayed at the nurse's words. The preparation for today's procedure has been distressing for Mum and upsetting to witness so the prospect of having to put her through it all over again is unthinkable.

Mum underwent the procedure a few weeks later, this time as an inpatient which made things a little easier and less upsetting. The second test revealed that she had polyps in her colon which fortunately did not require any further intervention. It was recommended that the test should be done again in three years' time however, the three of us were determined that, whatever the situation three years from now, there was no way Mum was going through that again.

19

SUNDAY DINNER

"Are we going anywhere today?" asks Mum.

"Yes Mum, we are going to Eleanor's for a nice roast dinner."

I put two Weetabix in a bowl and some milk in the microwave.

Mum is sitting at the kitchen table in her dressing gown awaiting her breakfast. I pour the warm milk over the Weetabix and drizzle them with honey.

"Are we going anywhere today?" She asks again.

"Yes, we are going to Eleanor's later," I say once more as I place her breakfast in front of her.

"There you are Mum." I take her hand to let her know where the bowl is. "I'm just making us a cup of tea. Eat your Weetabix before they get cold."

"Are we going out today?" she asks and again I tell her that we are going out for our dinner.

The kettle boils and I make the tea. Whilst Mum is eating her breakfast, the phone rings.

"Are we going out today?"

There is a knock at the door.

"Yes Mum, but not for a while yet."

I pick up the phone and ask the caller to wait a minute while I open the door. It's my little nephew who lives close-by. He skips inside proclaiming, "I've come to see Nanny."

He goes into the kitchen and holds up his latest superhero comic to show Mum. I tell Mum what he is showing her and she asks, "Are we going out today?"

I explain that little Mark is here, and he is showing her his comic. I try to engage Mum in a conversation with her Great-Grandson but she seems oblivious to his presence.

It breaks my heart to realise that little Mark will never know the joy of having Mum in his life.

"Oh shit," I mutter as I remember I have left somebody hanging on the phone. "Sorry, sorry, I forgot you were there," I tell the caller.

"It's OK," replies Iris. "I heard you speaking to someone, how is your mum today?"

"She's good, we're just having breakfast then I will get her ready. We're going to Eleanor's for dinner this afternoon."

Iris is always satisfied to learn that Mum has eaten and after a brief chat we finish the call and I return to the kitchen.

Mark runs to the fridge and takes out a yoghurt and looks up at me, waiting for permission to eat his favourite treat. I smile and hand him a spoon and am grateful that he is too little to understand the disregard his nanny has just demonstrated.

I sit with Mum and Mark at the table. We drink our tea and Mark finishes his treat then skips out shouting, "I'm going home now Nanny, I'll see you tomorrow."

I sit with Mum. She asks, "What's for breakfast?" then, "Are we going out today?"

I sigh and put some bread in the toaster when what I really want to do is scream at her to be quiet for just one bloody minute. We sit together with our tea and toast. It is barely 10:00am and I am already exhausted.

This constant repetition of the same question over and over has become a constant feature of Mum's behaviour and requires an enormous amount of patience. I have to admit it doesn't always come easily.

Eleanor and Jack are busy in the kitchen when we arrive at their home. Eleanor joins us in the lounge while Jack makes us all a cup of tea and tells us dinner will be about half an hour.

The three of us sit chatting while Jack finishes in the kitchen and we are soon tucking into the lovely meal he has prepared.

Later, when all four of us are sitting in the lounge, Mum asks, "Are we going out today?"

"You are already out Mum, remember Liz brought you to my house in a taxi so we could all have dinner together," Eleanor says.

"Did you enjoy your dinner Mum?" I ask.

She seems oblivious to my question. "Where are we?" She asks,

Eleanor explains we are in her house and have all just enjoyed our dinner, adding that Mum and I will be going back to her own house in a little while. Jack leaves the room and Mum looks up and moves her head around. She appears contemplative as she scans the room, not really taking anything in around her.

"Whose house is this?" she asks.

"It's my house Mum, you will be going back to your own house soon." Eleanor tells her.

I am sitting beside Mum on the settee and Eleanor is on the chair to her right when suddenly Mum asks, "Will Dennis be there when I get home?"

Her words strike me harder than any physical blow might have. My throat constricts and I cannot speak. I take hold of Mum's hand. I know Eleanor has a similar reaction as she is immediately beside Mum and takes her other hand. She too is silent for a moment; a sob escapes and I try hard to stem the tears which threaten. I still cannot speak.

Eleanor says in the gentlest of tones, "No Mum, he won't be there, remember Dad got really sick and died a few years ago."

Mum is silent for a beat then says, "That's right, cancer wasn't it?"

We sit in silence for several more seconds when Jack comes in from the kitchen having overheard the exchange. Jack always manages to come up with the right words at the most difficult times. He teases Mum about her forgetfulness and his words serve to soothe us all and we all manage a bit of a chuckle but the heart-breaking realisation of Mum's condition was never more profound than at that moment.

Mum seems not to have realised our distress and I am grateful for this small mercy but my sadness lingers, not only for Mum but for myself. Dad's death came only weeks after Mum's Alzheimer's diagnosis and some-times I feel like I have barely grieved for my dad as the enormity of Mum's needs following his death seem to have eclipsed everything else.

Although we rarely discuss our grief, I am fairly sure Eleanor and Jane feel likewise.

The months go by and after a prolonged battle with Social Services, Mum has been awarded additional care to meet her increasingly complex needs.

Although she remains physically fit and robust her Alzheimer's is progressing significantly and many aspects of her personality have changed forever. It is sometimes the smallest and most subtle changes which bring the most heartache, like the incident with the kettle or when it became apparent that she could no longer use the phone without help.

I have heard about the family of dementia sufferers being asked by their loved one, "who are you?" and I dreaded the day Mum might ask this of me, or perhaps say to me, "who was that?" when one of my sisters leaves the room.

I wonder how I would feel if this were to happen but, in the event, she never asks this of me; at least not in so many words.

She did ask me the question in a roundabout way.

The first time I remember it with any certainty was one Saturday afternoon during the summer of 2010. We were sitting tucking into an ice-cream courtesy of the ice-cream van which passed through Mum's street and always stopped at the end of her path.

I thought she was focusing on her ice-cream as she was very quiet for a few minutes, which was really unusual as her normal behaviour these days was to be constantly asking questions. Normally it would be the same question asked over and over again so these brief moments of silence were actually quite pleasant.

Out of the blue she asked, "What am I to you?"

A bit taken aback, I did not respond immediately. It took me several seconds to realise what had been said to me.

"You are my mum," I responded with authority. "You are my mum and I am your daughter."

She seemed to ponder my response but made no comment and appeared bewildered. In an attempt to lighten the moment and assuage my sadness, I went to sit beside her telling her, "you have three daughters but I am your favourite." I gave a chuckle to let her know this was meant as a joke and she responded in kind. I believed at that moment she understood my response was a bit naughty and wanted to acknowledge my humour.

Mum asked me the same question many more times over the next year or so until she eventually lost the ability to speak.

I always believed, and indeed still do, that even though she did not appear to know who we were; she understood on a deeper level that we did belong to her.

20

UNSEEN

Surely not again! This is the fourth time in ten minutes! I am muttering to myself and trying really hard to contain the frustration I am feeling right now. "Is she doing this on purpose because she knows how exhausted I am?" I say aloud, even though I am alone in my room. Don't be so bloody stupid! I tell myself.

I think the nonsense corralling around my head is just a symptom of my exhaustion and I try to shake off my weariness as, once again I help Mum to the bathroom.

This latest phase, whereby Mum feels the need to pee every couple of minutes (surely it is just a phase and please let it be a short-lived one!); began about four weeks ago.

Mum seems to be OK during the day when she mostly sits in her chair and potters around the house but when it comes to bedtime it's a whole different matter.

The usual routine is around 8:00pm when I make Mum her last cuppa of the day. This is always accompanied with a goody of some description; Mum has a sweet tooth and never refuses a cake or biscuit. Then, one by one, I give her the myriad of tablets she has been prescribed. Sometimes she takes them without any difficulty but more often than not she spits the tablet out or else does not take a sip of tea and starts to crunch the tablet instead. It is becoming increasingly difficult to have her take all the medication and the ritual can often take half an hour or more.

Once upstairs, Mum undresses and puts on her nightie. Sometimes she manages this herself, other times she needs help. I then take her into the bathroom and hand her a toothpaste-laden toothbrush. For some reason which I will never understand, brushing her teeth is something she manages well and is always very thorough. Ablutions done, we go into the bedroom and tuck her up in bed. I sit at the end of the bed for a few minutes, then go into my own room and get ready for bed myself.

Lately however, she has been in bed for a matter of minutes when she starts to shuffle about and shouts that she needs to pee. I once again help her to the bathroom and then back to bed. After the third trip to the bathroom I don't bother going into my bedroom. Instead I hover around her room and sure enough, up she gets again, claiming she needs to go to the toilet.

I speak to Eleanor and Jane; they too have experienced the same behaviour when they stay overnight. Eleanor tells me she has known her to be up ten times within the first hour of going to bed.

Once she settles and falls asleep she seems to be OK until morning but whatever the reason, the nighttime ritual takes its toll on me.

I am back at home a week later when Jane phones to let me know she and Eleanor are on their way to the Woman's Hospital with Mum.

When Molly had bathed Mum this morning, she noticed something odd down below.

"Something's not right," Molly told Jane, "I think Nanny needs to see a doctor."

The GP visited and said it looks as though she had a prolapsed bladder and immediately referred her to hospital. Jane promises to call me back when they return home.

Later when they are back at Mum's house Jane calls me and explains Mum does indeed have a prolapsed bladder. She has been fitted with a pessary which will hold the bladder in its correct place. Poor Mum, she must have been so uncomfortable but she never said a word. Just one more horrible aspect of this wretched disease! It seems to rob Mum of her ability to articulate anything and the prospect of her having suffered for weeks with this problem breaks my heart. An enormous sense of guilt seizes me as I remember how often I have bathed Mum recently and I am angry at not noticing this problem.

This is nonsense of course. There is no way I or either of my sisters could have seen what Molly had noticed, nevertheless, this is one of the very rare occurrences when my poor sight has left me 'mad as hell!' It was only when Molly, who does not have the family eye condition, bathed Mum that it came to light.

The nighttime ritual settles for a while. The pessary appears to have solved the problem and Mum seems to be physically well in all other aspects. The difficulty comes when, after a three month period, the pessary has to be replaced with a new one. This proves to be really traumatic for Mum.

She is uncooperative and struggles with the nurse who performs the procedure. Who can blame her; it is such an invasive and uncomfortable process and, not understanding what is going on, it is little wonder Mum fought against it.

21

WHY CHANGE NOW?

It is near the end of 2010, and tension between the three of us is beginning to appear with lots of niggles and disagreements becoming ever more frequent.

Eleanor and Jane are particularly affected by the stress and strain which five years of caring for Mum has brought and whilst we all agree that we want Mum to remain at home, it seems to be the only thing we do agree upon lately.

Eleanor has never been able to switch off from Mum's care, even when there are others looking after her. Eleanor is constantly worrying and phoning to make sure all is well.

Looking back, it was surprising that things went so horribly wrong at this particular time. Thanks to Jane's tenacity and perseverance when dealing with Social Services, Mum had a really good care package in place which included one of our cousins, Doris, who was now employed to look after Mum every Sunday and for several hours during the week.

Doris proved to be a tremendous help, often going over and above what was expected of her.

As Doris is now with Mum on a regular basis, it

prompts her sister, Rowena, to call in on Mum occasionally whilst Doris is there.

Rowena is a psychiatric nurse; she lives about a mile away from Mum and would often call into see Doris on her way home from a nightshift at the nursing home where she works.

One memorable incident came when Doris told Eleanor that we should not be giving Mum her Aricept in the morning. Doris has been told by her sister that this medication should be given at bedtime.

"She's been having the Aricept in the morning for the past five bloody years, why do we have to start giving them at night all of a sudden?" It's Jane on the phone she is angry and upset and I can only just about manage to understand what she is saying through her tears which seem to be more from anger and frustration rather than anything else.

Eleanor and Jane have been at loggerheads over the past few months. It seems like Eleanor is being influenced by Doris. To cut a long story short, it has become apparent that Doris has been discussing Mum's condition with Rowena.

OK, Doris and Rowena are both Mum's nieces but Doris is with Mum in an official capacity as a paid carer, and Rowena's visits to the house are for a social visit with her sister. It is fair to say that neither cousins visited Mum prior to Doris's employment.

Rowena has told Doris that Aricept should be given at night so we should change the medication regime. Jane is upset; she sees this as interference and is reluctant to make the change. She reminds me that when Mum was first prescribed Aricept, it was the consultant psychiatrist whom suggested that the tablet be administered in the morning.

I have to admit to being pretty angry myself at this development. Jane was right, there was no need for the change and I too felt it was interference which we could well have done without.

In an attempt to appease Jane and avoid antagonising Eleanor, who just seems to be angry about everything lately, I suggest that Jane should contact Mum's psychiatrist and ask whether there would be any problem with changing the time Mum was given the Aricept. By now Mum has been prescribed other medication so, if Aricept could indeed be introduced into the night time routine, then it is not worth herself getting worked up about.

The strain was beginning to take its toll on all three of us.

I remember being told in the early days by one of the psychiatric nurses, "some families fall apart whilst caring for a loved one with dementia; the strain often leads to family breakdown."

I thought at the time, thank goodness that will never happen to us, we are very close and all three of us are in agreement that Mum should remain in her own home, despite some professionals suggesting that Mum should go into residential care.

The discord between Eleanor and Jane is becoming ever more evident with Eleanor becoming increasingly critical of her. It soon becomes apparent that Eleanor is far from herself and both Jane and I are concerned she may be on the verge of a nervous breakdown.

Eleanor's behaviour at this time is completely out of character; she is bad-tempered and appears to be constantly angry and confrontational. It is so unlike her: actually, it is not in the nature of any of us to be confrontational. We are all fairly mild-mannered and easygoing but I suppose the strain we have all been under is just becoming too much for Eleanor who has not enjoyed particularly good physical health for several years.

Doris is forever phoning Eleanor with some niggle or other. Eleanor begins to dread a call from Doris which would often begin, "I have been talking to Rowena," which would often be followed with how we were getting things wrong. The Aricept incident was just one of many occasions when Rowena tried to interfere.

It was something which was not immediately apparent; we were so grateful to have Doris involved in Mum's care and we considered a family member who happened to be a psychiatric nurse could only be a benefit; we could never have imagined the nightmare which lay ahead.

Tension is increasing by the day and the atmosphere at Mum's is far from conducive to the provision of care we all want for her.

Iris has sensed that something is badly wrong and is constantly fretting about us, asking whether we are OK. Her concern seems to be focused on us, and in particular Eleanor, rather than Mum.

Doris and Rowena are our first cousins. Their mum was Mum's eldest sister who sadly died from cancer at just 52. Neither cousins, nor any of their four brothers, have the eye condition which affects us. They both drive and Doris often takes Mum out to visit Eleanor or Jane; sometimes she will just go for a drive with Mum if it is a nice day. Her overzealousness, however, nearly got her into a bit of a pickle.

Doris had agreed to deal with all of Mum's correspondence. Upon opening a phone bill, she noticed a particularly expensive call costing twenty-four pounds. She immediately advised Eleanor who was initially a bit flummoxed wondering why Doris felt the need to bother her with this as all Mum's bills were paid by direct debit so there was no need for any action regarding this particular bill.

Eleanor and Jane decide to check things out and with the help of the care register which was filled in daily by the carer who came in every morning to help bathe Mum. They establish that the only people in Mum's house at the time the call was made were Doris and Rowena. The call was made via the 118 118 facility so, at the time, there was no way of knowing from the bill to whom the call was made.

The entry in the register stated, 'bathed Annie with the help of Doris', thereby identifying Rowena as the person responsible for making the call.

Eleanor and Jane decide not to advise Doris of their findings in order to spare her embarrassment.

In a desperate attempt to alleviate the stress we decide that all three of us would have some time out from Mum's care, so we individually step out of the picture for a couple of weeks, managing the extra care between the remaining two.

Tension between Eleanor and Jane continues to escalate which all comes to a head one lovely spring afternoon in April 2011. I am at home when Jane phones in a state. She is crying as she explains she had been at Mum's house when Eleanor arrived. One word led to another and the two of them ended up having a ferocious slanging match in front of Mum, culminated with some shoving which left Jane bruised and badly shaken. Eleanor's daughter, Jade, was also there and did little to ease the situation. Eleanor stormed out leaving Jane in floods of tears with Mum wondering what was going on.

Jane told me later that Mum did not appear upset by the shouting, however, was fully aware of Jane's distress. Mum sat beside her asking her why she was crying; for want of something better to say she replied, "I am OK Mum, I just feel a bit sick."

Mum's response was to take her hand and say, "come on, I'll put you to bed."

Mum's kindly words and gestures served to soothe Jane and simultaneously sadden her as this tiny glimpse of the Mum we once had but was now lost only served to deepen her sorrow.

The tension over recent months has resulted in this terrible incident and upon learning of what has happened between my two sisters I feel a sense of absolute despair and utter helplessness.

What happens now, how can we get through this, I ponder. "Oh Mum I'm so sorry," I silently utter, "We are failing you."

I hardly have a chance to process everything when my phone rings again. It is Jane; she is a bit calmer and tells me that Iris, having heard about the incident, wants to speak to me so could I phone her? This I did and Iris's voice is laden with concern and confusion.

"What has been going on?" she asks.

The tears start to flow as they have a thousand times over the past few months.

Iris continues, "I knew things were difficult and you have all been under a lot of stress but I never imagined anything like this!"

I compose myself and tell her I will be at Mum's tomorrow so I will come and see her then.

I call Eleanor. Jack answers. He has instructions from her that she does not want to speak to anyone. I insist on talking to my sister and she eventually comes to the phone. She sounds broken, her voice is barely audible and I ask her how she is.

"I don't know," she whispers, "I don't know what to do. I can't bear it."

"I know, I know." I try to comfort her. "I don't know what to do either."

We are both silent for a while.

"Are you coming down?" she eventually asks.

I assure her I will be there in the morning and will call her as soon as I get to Mum's.

"I don't know what to do," she says again and once more all I can say is, "I know," because I really don't know what to do either.

The following morning I am at Mum's house. She is calm and seems to have no ill effects from the events of yesterday. Jane was with Mum when I arrived and has gone home for a while to see her family. She promises to come back in a little while so we can try to figure out where we go from here.

I really don't have a clue as to what to do for the best.

Mum and I are sitting quietly having a cup of tea when the doorbell rings. It is my three cousins, Doris, Rowena and their brother, Dickie. Having heard what has happened they say they have come to see whether they can help.

Doris produces a piece of paper and said, "We have come up with a new rota for the carers which might help ease the situation."

She goes on to outline the arrangements which mean juggling things around so that Doris no longer works Sundays and Rowena could be included as one of Mum's paid carers for two nights per week. The most alarming part of her proposal comes when she suggests things can be moved around so that Eleanor and Jane's paths would never have to cross.

My immediate thoughts are: you are not trying to help us, this is designed to benefit yourselves. Doris has been making noises over recent weeks about how she dislikes having to work on a Sunday and Rowena has been hinting to come on board as a paid carer. Rowena has made it known to us on a number of occasions that she dislikes her job in a residential nursing home and the proposal from Doris is designed so that Rowena can reduce her work hours in order to look after Mum.

Their suggestion also requires Molly to change the days she spends caring for my Mum in order to suit them.

I tell Doris I am not keen on their idea. I feel it is more important that my sisters and I sort out our differences so that we can give Mum our best attention without the stress we have all encountered over recent months.

It is obvious that Rowena is annoyed at my response as she stands up and storms toward the front door mumbling, "Well if you don't want my help," or words to that effect. Dickie persuades her to come back and sit down while we tried to sort things out.

Jane arrives which adds to the tension as she and Rowena have already had words a few weeks earlier when Rowena telephoned Jane one night to criticise her care of Mum. Apparently Jane and Molly had taken Mum out for lunch which Mum had paid for. How this got to Rowena's ears and more to the point, what the heck it had to do with her anyway, is another matter but Rowena thought it appropriate to phone Jane telling her how disgusting it was that Jane hadn't paid for the lunch herself. Her most outrageous comment was to say to Jane, "do you want me to put Keith, (her husband), on the phone to tell you just how disgusting you are?"

I remembered Jane phoning me in a right state following this call. I was outraged at Rowena's sheer audacity and wondered, what on earth was happening to my family, we seemed to be falling apart.

My three cousins leave after a short while. I thank them for coming, adding that we want to sort things out for ourselves.

Eleanor, Jane and I are at Mum's the following morning and after a lot of tears, regrets and apologies, we agreed that we will try to put the past few months behind us and find a way forward, for our own sake as much as Mum's.

By this time Eleanor has visited her GP as she is fully aware she is not coping well and is advised she is suffering from stress and anxiety. She has been prescribed a mild antidepressant and we decide that we really do need to take care of each other, not just Mum.

We agree that at the first sign of tension or difficulty from any of us, we will address the issue so that things will never become so unbearable again.

A couple of days later is the weekend of the Royal Wedding and Eleanor decides to celebrate William and

Kate's marriage at home with her family. Jane too has plans for something nice that weekend and I spend a few days in the Highlands with some friends.

It is a very rare occasion for all three of us to be absent from Mum, even for such a short period, however, safe in the knowledge that Mum is in good hands with other family members, all three of us make the most of the much needed respite.

A fragile truce exists between the three of us and our cousins, after all, they are family and Doris is a great help.

For a while we are walking on eggshells, trying not to say or do anything which may be taken the wrong way or cause upset. Slowly but surely things get back to normal, or at least what passes as normal in these difficult days, until later that year when a major change occurs in Mum's condition; one which impacts our lives in a way I wouldn't have thought possible.

22

GO TO BED

In August 2011 I am blessed with the arrival of my long awaited guide dog, Jeannie, a beautiful yellow Labrador/Retriever with the gentlest nature anyone could wish for.

Jeannie becomes my constant companion and improves my confidence no end.

Prior to her arrival I had been travelling back and forward between Liverpool and my home near Glasgow, using my white cane and as my sight deteriorated, with night blindness now a significant feature, the journey became increasingly difficult and a bit daunting.

Previously, I would have to plan my journeys carefully to ensure I would reach my destination before the daylight faded. During the winter months this severely limited my options for my travel arrangements but with Jeannie at my side, things became so much easier.

My training with Jeannie lasts around six weeks and precludes me travelling to see Mum. I had never been away from her for such a lengthy period and am anxious to get back to see her as soon as possible.

The first time I take Jeannie to Mum's house, Mum and Jeannie adopt an immediate bond which takes me by surprise. Jeannie will sit attentively beside Mum's armchair and the first time I help Mum upstairs to the bathroom, Jeannie waits patiently at the bottom of the stairs, wagging her tail awaiting my return, or so I thought. I walk downstairs a few paces ahead of Mum and to my utter surprise and delight, she ignores me as I reach the bottom step; instead she continues watching Mum until she is safely ensconced in her favourite armchair.

I am so happy and proud of Jeannie and I believe without a doubt, in that moment, my guide dog understands that Mum needs attention and responds accordingly.

The remainder of the visit is fairly uneventful. Eleanor and Jane both visit me; Mum and I take Jeannie to see Iris who instantly demonstrates a great fondness for Jeannie as we reminisce about Mum's various guide dogs and the difference they had made to her life.

I once asked Mum why Iris had never chosen to have a guide dog, Mum surprised me by saying she did not think Iris would be eligible for a dog because she had a history of mental health issues.

Everyone who applies for a guide dog is assessed individually and many people with additional health conditions have succeeded in training with a guide dog, including those with mental health conditions. Part of the assessment would be considering whether using a guide dog would make life easier or harder for the person, as each applicant is different and it is not 'one size fits all'.

I don't know whether Iris actually considered a guide dog herself, perhaps Mum's thoughts were just that she may just have assumed this was the reason. I thought it was a real shame that Iris had never enjoyed the benefits of having a guide dog although I am not sure whether it was through choice or otherwise.

Around the end of September 2011 Mum is scheduled to visit the Cherry Tree for her six monthly assessment. A new psychiatrist has been installed and he suggests that Mum should undergo an ECG to check there are no problems with her heart.

Eleanor questions the reason as Mum's physical health has never been an issue. The psychiatrist tells us it is just routine so the test is duly arranged.

"What are you talking about?" My tone is incredulous as I take in what Jane is telling me.

She repeats that Mum has been prescribed beta blockers and Aspirin.

"Why?" I ask. "What's wrong with her?"

"An irregular heartbeat," Jane responds.

I have my doubts about the need for this medication and indeed still do. As I have already said, Mum's physical health has never given cause for concern, but I suppose we have to accept that the doctors know best so the new medication was slotted into Mum's regime.

Within a week her condition changed so significantly that she would never leave the house again, or walk upstairs to her bedroom.

It is the first Sunday in October, 2011. I am at home when Jane phones. I can tell from her tone something is wrong. Jane tells me Mum has become very distressed over the last couple of days. She is reluctant to move from her armchair, and points to various parts of the room asking, "Who are those people over there?"

"It doesn't matter how many times I tell her there is nobody else here," Jane tells me, "She just seems afraid of something in the room."

I wonder whether Mum might have an infection again. We have learned over the years how this can lead to increased confusion and Mum has suffered a couple of urine infections in the last year or so. Jane says she will phone the doctor in the morning.

Antibiotics are prescribed and after the five-day course Mum's confusion is becoming more acute. She is having difficulty walking upstairs, not because of any physical problem; it is apparent she has literally forgotten how to lift one foot onto the bottom step in order to ascend.

Jane suggests that we should bring a single bed down into the lounge as she fears an accident will occur when attempting to get Mum upstairs at bedtime.

I travel to Mum's. By this time Jane has asked the GP to come and see Mum for himself. He suggests that the new medication might not agree with her and a different beta blocker is prescribed. The new tablets are immediately introduced but make no difference to Mum's increased confusion.

The day I arrive I notice that the lounge has been altered to accommodate the single bed. I am consumed with sadness as I realise yet another significant deterioration has occurred in Mum's condition.

Within less than two weeks a hospital bed is installed. The GP organises for a district nurse to visit Mum and Social Services arrange for additional carers to visit every day in order to cater for Mum's increased personal care needs now that she is bedridden.

It is now necessary to tend to all of Mum's bathing and all other aspects of personal hygiene, whilst she remains in bed.

We will learn soon afterwards that Mum was assessed as requiring palliative care.

By now Mum is really unwell; she is severely dehydrated and has a urine infection. There are times during the next few weeks when it looks like we are going to lose her.

The next three plus years see Mum's needs change completely. Gradually she loses the ability to feed herself and most of her meals have to be pureed and liquids thickened with a product called 'Thick & Easy, which I had never heard of. It is an odourless and tasteless powder which comes in a tin much like powdered baby milk, complete with measuring spoon.

Occasionally, when Mum is having a good day she will be sitting up in the hospital bed and can manage to hold a small piece of food and feed herself. Other times she literally has to be spoon-fed as you would a baby.

It is not too long after she becomes bedridden that Mum suffers her first Transient Ischaemic Attack (TIA), an interruption in the flow of blood to the brain; sometimes referred to as a 'mini stroke', which would become a regular feature throughout the remainder of Mum's life. She would be completely incapacitated by these episodes which would last anywhere between a few hours, to as much as a continuous period of thirty-six hours.

On one occasion in the early days of these episodes, we call the GP who advises that Mum's condition has probably changed from Alzheimer's, to vascular dementia and it is likely that the TIAs would become a regular feature of her condition.

My sisters and I begin to spend more and more time with Mum, remaining with her even when other carers are at her home.

There are some bizarre and distressing aspects to her condition over the next few years. She goes through a phase whereby she will lash out at whoever is bathing and changing her. Although she lost a considerable amount of weight and appears frail, her strength is incredible. I would often return home after a week or so spent at Mum's with scratches or bruises on my hands and arms. She even bit the back of my hand if I wasn't quick enough to get away from her grip.

I remember doing battle with her in the early hours of one morning; she had been particularly agitated and fidgety for many hours and I had not had any sleep for the past two nights so was exhausted and more than a bit frustrated with her.

I stood beside her bed as she was flailing her arms and wriggling around the bed. Concerned that she would hurt herself, I tried to hold her arms still; it was a battle of wits who was going to give up the struggle first and in my frustration, I took a tight hold of both her hands and shouted, in a less than friendly tone, "For pity's sake, will you just go to sleep!"

The words were hardly out of my mouth when I just hung my head and sobbed. Through my tears I told Mum, "I'm sorry, I'm sorry, I didn't mean to shout at you."

I don't remember ever feeling so guilty and wretched; I could hardly believe I had spoken to Mum, my lovely mum, in this way.

She becomes doubly incontinent and this proves to be a particularly distressing thing to witness and difficult to manage. Often she will haul at her incontinence pad, tearing it away and spreading excrement around the bed, over her hands and even through her hair.

One very scary symptom presents itself about a year later. She begins to experience 'secretions,' accumulation of saliva in the back of her throat which she cannot clear for herself and which can cause episodes of choking. We often have to call in a nurse when the secretions are particularly bad, other times, lying Mum on her side will be enough to allow the accumulated fluid to flow out of her mouth.

23

RIP IT UP

Oh God I am so tired, Mum has become restless and in my semiconscious state I silently beg her to settle down and go back to sleep. A futile plea I know but it gives me an extra precious moment in my make-shift bed.

I hear groans followed by the all too familiar ripping sound which lets me know Mum is tearing at the bedclothes with her teeth. She began this peculiar phase about six weeks ago and it is becoming ever more frequent, she has quite literally reduced duvet covers and nighties to shreds.

There is only one thing to do at such times and I unwrap the fleecy blanket which cocoons me as I move to Mum's side; taking her hand.

"Come on now Mum try not to do that." It takes a monumental effort for me to talk to Mum in a soft, conciliatory tone.

I shake off the overwhelming weariness and take her hand; she bunches up a corner of duvet cover and tries to put it to her mouth. I am holding her hand in an attempt to halt its progress, her strength never fails to surprise me.

It's 2:43am. I try and shuffle into a comfortable position on the chair at her bedside whilst maintaining a firm but gentle grip on Mum's hands. The tugging continues. I long to lie down and close my eyes but Mum cannot be left, even for a moment when she is in this state. The main concern is that a thread of material could choke her or the biting could break a tooth which also could cause her to choke. These concerns aside, it is so upsetting to see her in such an agitated state and there is no way I could not be close by to offer whatever comfort I can.

The doctors and nurses who are involved in Mum's care are baffled by this behaviour and have no answers as to how best manage it. The myriad of medication tried over recent weeks has little to no effect.

We are forever hearing, "You're doing a great job, just carry on as you are." The words offer little comfort as we witness our Mum's suffering.

Mum's agitation increases and it becomes ever more difficult to prevent her tearing the bedclothes without a considerable amount of effort. I am terrified of hurting her and simultaneously angry; for what, I don't know, I just know I am.

My throat constricts and I clamp my teeth together. I find I am doing this a lot lately and think I am trying to prevent the frustration and anguish I feel, escaping from my mouth.

I sit beside Mum for ten minutes, or is it an hour? It's hard to know; time has no relevance just now. Mum's agitation begins to ease and I release my breath which I didn't realise I was holding. I wait for several moments until I think she has drifted off.

"Please, please, please," I silently utter as I slowly remove my hand from Mum's grip. I stand over her, barely daring to breathe lest I disturb and awaken her; when I tiptoe back to the couch I check the clock, it is 4:55am.

I wrap up in the fleecy blanket and try to doze off. Wouldn't you know, Mum is snoring and I am now wide awake; my weariness of a few hours ago has disappeared and I just lie there listening to the dawn chorus and waiting for the new day to begin. Perhaps today will be a better day?

24

A DIFFICULT YEAR

In January 2013, Eleanor and Jack are preparing to go on holiday to celebrate Eleanor's birthday.

The night before they are due to leave, Eleanor has a serious fall at home, breaking her wrist and hip.

She requires emergency surgery involving a hip replacement and a metal plate put into her arm.

She remains in hospital for several weeks and following her discharge requires intensive physiotherapy.

A few days after she returns home from hospital, Mum suffers a particularly severe TIA. Doris is with Mum that particular morning and Rowena has popped in to see her sister as she often does on her way home from a night shift.

Doris is concerned that Mum was not too good and calls Jane to say she should come straight away. Jane does not let Eleanor know about Mum's condition as Eleanor is housebound, recovering from her surgery.

When Jane arrives, Mum is listless and appears barely conscious. Rowena takes charge of things, examining Mum closely whilst Jane sits at the other side of the bed, holding Mum's hand.

Rowena proclaims, "She's gone," to no one in particular.

Her words prompted Jane to cry out, "No, no," at which point Mum rallied, letting out a moan.

"You've brought her back Jane," Rowena proclaimed.

Still concerned about Mum's condition, Doris telephones Eleanor and suggests she should come up right away.

Eleanor is still incapacitated at this time and it takes a considerable amount of effort to get her into a taxi and travel to Mum's bedside.

I too travel to my Mum's house following a conversation with Rowena who tells me Mum is very poorly. After a few days her condition improves slightly and Eleanor returns home to continue her recuperation whilst Jane and I remain with Mum for a while longer.

Later that same year, Eleanor becomes seriously ill and is admitted into hospital with kidney failure.

It is late July and once again she and Jack have a holiday booked; this time with two of their grandchildren.

For the second time in just six months Eleanor misses out on a holiday owing to illness. I know! You couldn't make it up.

Poor Eleanor, she has not had much luck with her health over recent years. Following what she thought would be a quick visit to her GP for a persistent cough, she is referred to a cardiologist and diagnosed with an aortic stenosis, the abnormal narrowing of a passage to the aortic valve.

Eleanor is initially advised that, although her condition is not too serious, she will have to be monitored every year to check her condition has not worsened.

Eleanor regularly attends the cardiologist for approximately four years following the initial diagnosis and is advised on each occasion that all is well, however there may come a time in the future when surgical intervention is required.

About a year before this diagnosis, Eleanor required a lengthy stay in hospital due to an exceptionally low haemoglobin count; this diagnosis too came following a routine blood test to check on her diabetes. The day after the blood test she was summonsed back to her GP who said she needed to be admitted immediately to hospital. She required three blood transfusions and underwent a colonoscopy, endoscopy and a myriad of blood tests as the doctors feared the unusually low haemoglobin level may be the result of internal bleeding.

She remained hospitalised for eleven days and was eventually discharged requiring long-term medication, including B12 injections every three months, but no specific diagnosis or reason for the dangerously low blood reading.

It seemed like if there were to be any serious health issues in the family, Eleanor would be on the receiving end.

Considering the serious nature of many of her illness's, Eleanor's resilience and determination seems to know no bounds and she always surprises everyone with her remarkable ability to bounce back.

I can only recall one occasion when Eleanor and her husband Jack were utterly devastated when ill-health befell their family.

This time it was not Eleanor who became unwell; instead her son, John, suffered a stroke, or so it was initially thought, at the age of twenty five.

Following a lengthy stay in hospital and a myriad of tests, including two spinal punctures, a particularly painful and uncomfortable procedure in which fluid is collected from the spine, John was diagnosed with Multiple Sclerosis (MS).

This was a particularly cruel blow as John is the only one of Eleanor's three children affected by the family eye condition.

John was studying Sociology and Social Policy at the University of Liverpool when he became unwell and was forced to abandon his studies for a year.

In spite of the difficulties he encountered owing to his poor sight coupled with the bolt out of the blue when he was diagnosed with MS, he returned to his studies the following year and upon completion was rewarded with a Bachelor of Arts 2.1 degree.

The day of his graduation was one of the happiest and proudest moments for our family. John had overcome enormous difficulties and, not content with his achievement, went on to study for a further year which brought a Masters.

Perhaps he gets his resilience and strength of character from Eleanor, who knows!

25

HONEY, HONEY

Mum continues to experience TIAs and we begin to realise this is just the way it will be from now on.

We are fully aware that the time will come when she won't recover from one of these episodes but we cannot afford to dwell upon this; all we can do for her is to be there and keep her as comfortable as possible.

There were some really dark times during the period Mum was bedridden and sometimes it was impossible to imagine the happy and carefree family we had once been.

Brief moments of sheer delight did present themselves however and when they did, my goodness, the depth of relief and absolute joy eclipsed everything in that moment.

I can recall with such clarity the night my lovely mum awoke from a thirty-six hour semi-comatose state.

I wrap myself in the fleecy blanket and try to sleep.

I am so cosy; Mum is silent and very still – too still really. The carer has not long left and between us we make Mum comfortable, changing her pad and freshening her face and hands whilst trying not to disturb her too much. We turn her so she is lying on her right side. More often than not, Mum would shuffle around during the course of the night. Tonight however, she will probably remain perfectly still as she normally does whilst having one of these awful episodes.

The past thirty-six hours have been really scary. Mum seems to have had a turn as we have come to refer to these episodes which are becoming ever more frequent.

We called the GP in yesterday and, as on previous occasions, he told us there was nothing to be done except keep Mum comfortable and when she comes round, give her as much to drink as possible.

I don't know why we called the doctor as we know there is nothing he can do for her but his visits offer us some comfort and reassurance.

It's only just after 9:00pm but the last couple of days have been exhausting and the worry and strain are taking their toll. My entire body aches and I long to lie down. I have come to realise that sleep should be grabbed with both hands when the opportunity arises. I am only a few feet away from Mum's bed and I know I will awaken if she begins to stir.

I hear noise in the distance. I ignore the sound until I remember where I am. I wake with a start, as I realise it is Mum muttering and fidgeting. I am immediately on my feet and at her bedside.

"Hello sleepy head," I exclaim, "Where have you been?"

I am so overwhelmed with joy that she has come round and seems to have suffered no ill effects from her catatonic state. She begins to rally and becomes animated, wriggling onto her back. I take the remote control and arrange the bed so that she is sitting up.

"Hey Mum," I say as I stroke her forehead and I cannot contain my joy, she is back and I smile to myself.

"How would you like something to drink? Silly question, of course you would you must be parched." I answer my own question. Mum lost the ability to speak some time ago.

I go into the kitchen and pour some cranberry juice into a beaker which I thicken with Thick & Easy and spoon-feed Mum with the cold drink. All of Mum's drinks now have to be thickened as she can no longer swallow liquids.

She devours the drink and I make her another which she takes with equal relish. I know how important fluids are and when she has been barely conscious for days at a time, any opportunity to give her as much to drink as possible is really important.

I ask Mum whether she would like some toast. "You must be starving," I say, expecting no response.

I put two slices of bread into the toaster which I spread with honey. I take the plate of toast, a flannel and towel and place them on the cabinet at Mum's bedside. I freshen her face and hands with the damp flannel. She is wide awake by now and I fold one of the slices of toast and place it in her hand; she immediately lifts it to her mouth and bites off a large chunk of the soft honey-laden toast. I help her break it into a more manageable size and she munches away as though she hasn't eaten in days, which of course she hasn't.

When she finishes and is left with only the dry crust I try to take this from her so that I can give her the next piece.

She has a tight grip on the crust and is determined not to part with it. I explain that I have another piece for her but of course she doesn't understand.

"Come on Mum, give that to me."

Something seems to register with Mum; she hesitates for a moment as if pondering my words. What happens next reduces me to tears.

Mum slowly and very deliberately, takes the crust between both hands and breaks it in half. She immediately pops one piece into her mouth and hands the other piece to me mumbling something which I swear was, "Here you are."

I quickly realise without a doubt that Mum thinks I want the toast crust for myself and, even though she must be starving, is willing to sacrifice her last bite for me.

It takes me a moment to compose myself. I give her the remainder of the toast, followed by a yoghurt.

Mum appears content as she shuffles herself down the bed. I just stand beside her smiling with tears of joy cascading down my cheeks as I take her hand and whisper, "Oh Mum, you're still in there aren't you?"

I return to the couch where I silently weep.

My emotions right now are impossible to define. My tears of joy at Mum's emergence from the coma-like state conflict with the endless sadness at how much of Mum has been lost forever.

26

THE CALM BEFORE THE NIGHTMARE

A fairly settled period follows Eleanor's turbulent year and even though Mum is deteriorating, there seems to be an element of calm within the family. We all determined that we will be with her at every opportunity.

Iris too seems to accept Mum is really poorly and will come and sit beside her sister often. It is such a sad site. Iris will just sit beside Mum holding her hand and barely speaking.

Mum is oblivious to Iris which I think must be so difficult for her as, for so long, Iris was reluctant to accept Mum's illness and is just beginning to realise that Mum will probably not be with us for much longer.

Iris, like Mum, has always enjoyed good physical health however, the three of us have been particularly worried about some peculiar aspects of her behaviour over recent years.

Eleanor alerts Doris and Rowena to her concerns, after all, Iris is their auntie too, but her pleas for help fall upon deaf ears.

PART THREE

27

WHERE DO I BEGIN?

I barely know where to begin.

Iris's story is so incredibly complex, it is difficult to know how best to relay her story with all its peculiarities without distracting from the wonderful, caring and sometimes, unbelievably frustrating person we were fortunate to have as our auntie.

As a little girl I remember with such clarity spending many happy hours in the small flat Iris and Henry shared close to our home in Brookvale.

One of my favourite memories was sitting browsing through an old Black Magic chocolate box which was filled with family photographs, one special black and white picture of a young Iris and two other very glamorous ladies wearing long floaty dresses and each with a corsage wristband displaying a contestant number.

I loved hearing the story behind the picture. Iris had come third in a beauty contest.

Uncle Henry, who was forever kidding around and telling crazy stories, said, "She would have come first except she was hit by a bus on the way to the contest and it spoiled her looks."

It was Iris and Henry who took Jane and me to see our very first movie, 'The Sound of Music', showing in

Liverpool in the mid-sixties. Another memorable adventure was to a bowling alley not far from our home in the city. This time it was Eleanor and I who were taken out and were thrilled to be given a whole knickerbocker glory each – what a treat!

During the few months when our auntie and uncle still lived in Liverpool after we had moved to Brookvale, Eleanor or I would often go to stay with Iris when Henry was working a nightshift.

We would always wake up to find a bar of chocolate under our pillow which had been placed there by our uncle on his return home. He would sneak into the bedroom and put the chocolate there before we awoke.

Our childhood was peppered with such indulgences.

My sisters and I continued to enjoy special days out with treats and gifts bestowed upon us throughout our childhood and beyond. I used to think how lucky we were to have such a brilliant auntie and uncle.

To the best of my knowledge, Iris never worked following her marriage in August 1954 which was fairly normal for many women of her generation, choosing to remain at home which she kept immaculate and which I always thought of as 'very posh.'

I loved hearing stories from her younger days, particularly when she talked about the times she and my mum and two of their other sisters were evacuated to North Wales during the war.

Even at the age of ten or eleven one story really bothered me and made me wonder whether the evacuees had been given a bit of a hard time by some of their hosts.

Iris recounted how one particular night enemy planes were flying over the sparsely populated village which was her temporary home, on their way to bomb Liverpool. Iris had become frightened and sought comfort from her host mother only to be told, "It's OK, they are not interested in us; it's Liverpool they are after."

I remember thinking how insensitive her words were to the young Iris whose parents and two siblings were still in Liverpool at the time.

I was often regaled with stories about romantic walks on secluded beaches when, in their younger days, Iris and Henry enjoyed many happy holidays on the Isle of Man and Guernsey. I thought this sounded like a boring pursuit as my own childhood holidays were to lively caravan parks and fairgrounds. I now fully appreciate her love for this type of holiday as I too now enjoy tranquil times in quiet countryside.

Sometime around the middle of 1976, my mum discovered that an eye specialist in Switzerland, a Professor Bangetta, claimed to be able to help save and, in some cases, improve the sight of people with Retinitis Pigmentosa (RP). The degenerative disease of the retina which ultimately results in total sight loss. In most cases, it is the peripheral vision which is lost first leaving the sufferer with what is often referred to as 'tunnel vision'. My family however, just to be difficult, have 'A Typical' RP and it is our central vision which is initially lost.

Perhaps this accounts for the late diagnosis and confusion between specialists when we were younger, as to the exact cause of the condition affecting such a large proportion of my family.

Mum made it her mission to find out more about the treatment and how she could get us to Switzerland for this remarkable opportunity.

By that time Mum, Iris and their elder sister Dolly had virtually lost all of their sight and Eleanor, Jane and I, along with Dolly's daughter Jess and son Ben, had various degrees of sight loss with Ben having the least sight of the five cousins; an oddity considering he was the youngest of us all. Just another peculiarity of the disease affecting my family.

For my part, I could hardly believe my sight could be improved, after all, we had had a lifetime of hearing, "there is no cure for your condition," so even though by nature I am a fairly positive and optimistic person; the prospect of my mum and her sisters being able to see and the rest of us not losing any more sight, seemed too good to hope for so whilst I was excited, I remained a bit cautious.

Iris however, went all out, over the top with childlike awe and enthusiasm.

One memorable conversation with Iris which worried me slightly took place shortly before we were ready to travel to Switzerland; she was excited at the prospect of a whole new lease of life once she had her sight back.

She wanted to get a job, she told me. "Maybe I could work in an office like you?"

Another of her plans was to learn to drive. There was no doubt in her mind that the Swiss treatment would be nothing short of a miracle.

I did not want to burst her bubble by expressing my own thoughts.

After almost a year spent finding out more about the treatment, raising sufficient funds to cover travel, accommodation for the four weeks we would have to attend the clinic, as well as the hospital fees; and generally liaising with various specialists in this country and abroad, we were finally all set to make the exciting, not to mention emotional, journey to the Opos Clinic in St Gallon, Switzerland in May 1977.

Following two days of examination by various specialists at the clinic, we were all gathered in a comfortable lounge area as the professor, together with some of his colleagues, explained his findings and what he was able to do for some of us.

It took a while to take in everything; there was a fair amount of medical jargon used and of course the language barrier had to be overcome, but the upshot was, Mum, Iris and Dolly did not have sufficient sight remaining to make the complex treatment viable. Perhaps more distressing was that Ben too had so little sight that he might not be a suitable candidate for the treatment. Further tests were required to confirm this.

Finally, on day three, Eleanor, myself, Jane and Jess all started the gruelling and painful procedures involving an injection directly into each eye, every day except Sunday, for a period of three weeks followed by a relatively minor operation to implant a tiny membrane into the back of the eye. Each injection as well as the surgical procedure was carried out under local anaesthetic so to say the process was uncomfortable was a bit of an understatement.

Ben started his treatment a couple of days after the rest of us to the great relief of us all, especially his mum and Jess.

At some point during our visits to the clinic which we attended every day as outpatients, Mum confessed that she had been relieved to hear she would not be undergoing the treatment as the prospect of being poked and prodded like a pin cushion, as she put it, terrified her. She was genuinely overwhelmed and delighted that we were going to benefit from the experience. Dolly too seemed to be of similar mind, especially when Ben was deemed suitable to proceed.

On the other hand, Iris seemed devastated upon hearing the news and went very quiet for the longest time. I can clearly remember feeling so sorry for my auntie who looked as though her world had been shattered.

We travelled to Switzerland once more the following year for a further round of treatment.

It is difficult to measure the success or otherwise of this venture as all of us cousins have subsequently lost our sight. What I can say with absolute certainty is, I did retain some useful sight for far longer than my mum and her siblings so, if it did nothing else, the Swiss treatment definitely slowed down the progress of the disease and for that, I remain eternally grateful.

28

EPISODES

Things started to go horribly wrong for Iris around the early Eighties. Her marriage became strained and she began to display worrying signs of something being not quite right.

She was forever visiting her GP with some imagined problem; on one memorable occasion she shaved her head, convinced that she had an infestation of lice. Another occasion when she was home alone one Sunday evening she telephoned an ambulance claiming, "I need to be in hospital, I think I am dying."

Mum and Dolly and I rushed to the hospital immediately upon hearing the news only to be told Iris was in good physical health however she was to remain in hospital overnight and would be seen by a psychiatric doctor the following day.

She was discharged with no specific diagnosis after just a couple of days and continued to visit her doctor with some ailment or other until eventually, her long standing GP refused to keep her on his books and she reluctantly joined the same practice as my mum.

I remember Mum and her other siblings being really worried about their sister's peculiar behaviour and sadly, Iris was sectioned under the Mental Health Act on 24 February 1986.

She remained hospitalised for many weeks with a diagnosis of paranoia and psychosis.

The next few years saw Iris straddling between the auntie we had known and loved throughout our entire lives and the barely recognisable introverted and confused individual she sometimes became.

The family was dealt a horrific and desperately sad blow in April 1989, when our cousin Ben, who was studying music at a college for the blind in Hereford, died suddenly from a brain aneurism, at the age of just 28.

Naturally, Dolly and Jess were completely devastated. Dolly had been widowed at a fairly young age so this second cruel blow seemed so unfair. Iris too was particularly affected by Ben's loss; her grief was obvious and was only eclipsed by her concern for Dolly and Jess.

Sadly, Uncle Henry suffered a fatal heart attack in September that same year at the age of 58 and whilst the three of us were devastated at the sudden loss of our beloved uncle, Iris seemed nonplussed, displaying little emotion.

A little over a year after being widowed, she moved into the house next door but one from our family home, and just two doors away from Dolly; three blind sisters now occupied three of the four terraced houses in the small street where I had grown up.

In February 1991, my dad suffered a serious heart attack which required a long stay in intensive care followed by several weeks in a cardiac ward and during this difficult period for Mum and the three of us, Iris could not have been more supportive and caring, although it was notable that she did not visit Dad in hospital.

During the first four nights of Dad's illness, we were allowed to stay in the family room next to the intensive care unit and it was Dolly who insisted on staying with us; she wanted to be near Mum to offer whatever comfort she could.

When the three of us remember this frightening period when Dad's condition was critical, we always smile as we recount that, even if we had been able to get a bit of sleep in that uncomfortable room, Dolly's snoring, which we likened to a foghorn, would have put a stop to that.

Dad eventually made a good recovery although he was never fit enough to return to work in a local engineering firm so retired at the age of 59.

The next few years were fairly uneventful as we focused on Dad's recovery. Iris was fairly settled, demonstrating no particular cause for concern until a troubling incident in July 2005. There was a large renovation project being undertaken by the local housing authority and Iris was due to have a new kitchen installed around this time. She had made it known that she dreaded the upheaval and did not want strangers in her home.

Shortly before the work was to start, Iris had a minor accident at home when she stumbled near the bottom of the stairs, hurting her foot. When my mum and dad went to see how she was, Iris insisted she was OK and refused medical attention claiming she just needed to rest her foot.

Eleanor and Jane visited Iris to see how she was and were told that she would be living downstairs for a while as she found it difficult getting around and couldn't manage the stairs. She cancelled the proposed renovation work claiming she was not fit to cope with the upheaval.

She gave Jane her front door key telling her to leave it in Mum's house so any visitors could let themselves in and she said she needed one of them to come in every day to make her meals and attend to her needs. Up until this point, Eleanor and/or Jane visited Iris every second day taking her to the local shops. Other visitors included Dolly and Mum and Dad. Eleanor and Jane's children often popped in to see Iris too, otherwise she had very few visitors to her home.

Despite having several other nieces and nephews who all lived nearby, she had little to no contact from any of them. Her only other visitor was a niece on her late husband's side, Pauline.

During the ensuing three months Iris continued to live downstairs, asking for wet wipes to be added to her shopping which she used instead of bathing. She requested ready meals for easiness; Eleanor or Jane would go in every day and make up sandwiches or snacks for her evening meal and heat up the ready meal which Iris ate at lunchtime. They would also prepare hot and cold drinks to be left for Iris as and when she wanted them.

One particular task they were asked to do every single day was to take a black bin bag wrapped up and tied tightly to the outside bin, this was as well as the usual detritus from the waste bin in the kitchen.

Eleanor and Jane each had family holidays planned during this period so, to ensure one or the other was not left alone to care for Iris every day, I travelled to Mum and Dad's on a number of occasions, staying for several days on each visit so that I could help out.

On one occasion Jane forgot to take the front door key back into Mum's house so the following day she had to knock on the door and shout through the letterbox that she didn't have the key. Iris eventually opened the door and was scathing in her greeting, stating she had to drag herself to the door because of Jane's stupidity. Jane did what Iris asked and ensuring that she had the key this time, she left. Jane was so distressed at Iris's rebuke coupled with the strain of caring for her under such difficult circumstances, she went straight home in floods of tears, not going into Mum's house as my dad was not very well and she did not want him to see her in such a state.

On the way home she telephoned Pauline to tell her about the situation with Iris. Pauline telephoned Jane later that night to say she had spoken to Iris on the phone and was going to call in on her but Iris had told her not to bother as she would have to call at Annie's house first to collect the key and as Dennis was not very well, she did not want him disturbed.

Pauline told Jane that Iris sounded fine.

Jane was upset by the incident, particularly as both she and Eleanor had previously advised Doris and Rowena about the situation with their auntie, and apart from coming to see Iris for a brief visit, they did nothing to help. Rowena's only contribution was to say to Jane, "If she wants to shit in a bucket, let her."

This brings me back to the black bin bag situation. Eleanor had become concerned that the bin bags contained the sandwiches which were made and left for Iris on a daily basis. She was worried that, apart from the ready meal, Iris was not eating anything else. Eleanor decided to check this out and instead of throwing the black bag into the bin she took it to our mum's house to examine the contents; she was horrified to find the bag contained masses of damp toilet paper and the contents of a bucket which had been used as a toilet.

Eleanor had advised Doris and Rowena of this, hence the comment from Rowena about shit in a bucket.

This situation continued for a total of three months putting considerable strain and distress on Eleanor and Jane; our dad seemed to be increasingly tired and just not himself and the three of us were finding things ever more stressful. Particularly when Dad, usually so mild mannered and easy going, became upset and angry at the situation exclaiming, "Iris has plenty of other nieces, they should be helping." He was right of course but, like I said, none of them bothered with Iris.

Around the middle of October my sisters decided the situation could not continue and reluctantly went to see Iris's GP who came to see her the following day, much to her dismay. Eleanor and Jane were given a severe roasting from Iris and a lecture from Mum, however the doctor upon examining Iris said she was physically and mentally OK and should start to move around the house in order to get her mobility back.

The three of us continued to go into Iris's every day helping her to walk around the house; by the end of October she was fully mobile and able to get up and down the stairs. Some aspects of her life changed forever at this point. She never again went to the shops whereas beforehand she went out with Eleanor or Jane a few times a week and was well known to staff.

On 8 November 2005 our dad was diagnosed with cancer, a day which is indelibly printed in the mind of all three of us and it is for this reason I can pinpoint so accurately, the time of this worrying episode with Iris.

29

TROUBLING TIMES

During Dad's illness Iris was always there for us, albeit from the confines of her home.

When Dad passed away in April 2006, Iris attended the funeral service but insisted on being taken straight home afterwards rather than attending the wake. For many years, perhaps even decades, she had deplored alcohol and would not go anywhere where it was being served.

For several years Iris seemed to be fairly settled and gave no real cause for concern until around 2011 when she began to complain that her mail was being interfered with and money as well as various items, including underwear, were being stolen from her home.

Other truly bazaar incidents became ever more frequent over the following years. Eventually Jane turned to the CPN who attended Mum.

Iris was eventually diagnosed with dementia and paranoid psychosis, a particularly sad development no more so than because Iris was so very alone by this time; Mum was now bedridden with no ability to communicate and Dolly had been admitted into a nursing home following a dementia diagnosis in 2008.

My sisters and I muddled through, helping her as much as was physically possible. Her needs were demanding more and more of our time and we did what we could whilst continuing to care for our mum.

As before, Eleanor and Jane continued to raise their concerns about Iris to Doris and Rowena, however there were no offers of help or concern from any of our cousins for their blind, widowed, childless auntie.

Molly began taking care of Iris's shopping and reading her mail sometime around early 2011. Previously it was Eleanor who did the majority of her shopping etc but with her failing sight and poor health Eleanor was unable to cope with the increasingly stressful and difficult demands Iris made upon her.

As had been the case for many years, her bank statements and any financial correspondence were always kept very close to her chest. She was incredibly private when it came to her finances and received her bank statements in audio form – an old-fashioned cassette which she listened to on an archaic cassette player.

Not only was Doris fully informed about the increasingly frequent and distressing aspects of our auntie's behaviour, she did indeed witness such an incident whilst working at Mum's house.

It happened one morning when Doris was in the back garden at Mum's house, hanging out some washing. Doris told Eleanor that she had witnessed Iris shouting out of her bedroom window to the neighbour who lived between her and Mum.

Doris was upset when recounting the incident; apparently Iris was shouting and swearing to Fred, the neighbour, to "get out of my fucking garden," along with other profanities. Fred was nowhere to be seen.

Iris had been complaining for some time that her neighbour had been going into her garden and cutting the grass.

Another neighbour who lived opposite her had told us that she had witnessed Iris tipping buckets of water over the front lawn.

When challenged she responded, "Fred brings his electric mower into my garden and this will sort him out, he will get electrocuted!"

I witnessed many similar disturbing aspects of her behaviour which became more frequent and if anything, even more bazaar during 2012 and 2013.

I was at Mum's for a long period in May 2012 and went into Iris's each day as she seemed to be particularly distressed, insisting that her mail was being intercepted and money was going missing from her bank account. Molly confirmed that Iris had been making more withdrawals than usual over recent weeks and Jane had spoken to the CPN about this relatively new trait.

It was apparent that she was seriously concerned about her finances, insisting that someone was stealing her money. I persuaded her to contact the police. She seemed reluctant but eventually agreed that it was probably for the best.

My reason for wanting to involve the police was not because I thought she was being robbed; it was because I believed that the police could look into her concerns and put her mind at rest once and for all.

Two police officers visited her on 21 May 2012 and, knowing she was blind, had suggested she should have a sighted family member present when they visited. Iris requested that Molly could be there to help.

To cut a long story short, after several hours going through Iris's bank accounts the police concluded that there was nothing amiss and all monies were accounted for after the discovery of a substantial amount of cash was found in her kitchen drawer, which she did not realise was there.

Just a couple of months after the incident with the police, I was at Mum's asleep on the couch when I was awakened by a knock at the door. I became very concerned when I realised it was around 2:30am. As it was just Mum and I in the house I was reluctant to open the door so I shouted to ask who was there. A female voice responded, "Its Michelle from across the road, your relative is out on her path shouting and swearing."

At this point I could hear Iris shouting. I thanked Michelle and while she was there Iris went inside and slammed her door. I immediately phoned Iris asking whether she was alright. She was very abrupt in her response. I chatted with her and she assured me there was nothing wrong; I reminded her of the time and suggested that she should go to bed.

I remained at the front door for several minutes to listen for any further activity from Iris's house. After a short while her door opened and she started to shout that someone had stolen her keys. I shouted to let her know I was there. I told her it was the middle of the night and she should go inside. This she did. I phoned her again and she appeared a bit calmer at this point and we chatted for a while until I was satisfied that she was OK and would be going to bed.

On another occasion Iris phoned around 8:00pm and said, "Someone has been in my house and left stuff in the kitchen cupboard."

I asked what sort of stuff. She could not explain but was adamant there was stuff in the meter cupboard which did not belong to her so somebody must have been in and put it there. I was alone with my mum who was awake and a bit agitated so could not be left alone. I phoned Jane who immediately came up in a taxi with her husband Paul who looked after Mum whilst I went into Iris's house; she showed me the cupboard which had some bags of plaster and tiles in it. I looked around the rest of the house to make sure nothing was out of the ordinary and satisfied that all was OK I returned to Mum's and told Jane what I had found. Jane told me Iris had had new taps and wall tiles fitted in her kitchen a week ago, presumably the material in the cupboard had been left by the council workmen who had carried out the work.

Another occurrence was when the police were called by a concerned neighbour in the middle of the night to report Iris who was out on her path in her dressing gown shouting and screaming. I believe the police reported this incident to Social Services.

On one of the very rare occasions when Iris visited Mum I took her home around 5:00pm. Later that evening she phoned me insisting that someone had been in her house whilst she had been out. She continued, "They have been in my underclothes drawer and taken some of my things."

I asked her to check the back door was locked. She assured me that it was and the safety chain was on the front door. I asked her to open the door as I was coming in to see her. She reluctantly agreed and I went in and found nothing unusual; the backdoor was locked and nothing seemed out of order. I asked if she wanted to come into Mum's, but she declined saying she was fine. I did not stay long as Mum was alone in her house.

In recounting these desperately sad episodes, it is easy to think that Iris shuffled from one crisis to another. The truth however, is that often weeks and even months would pass with no such incidents. Whilst her reclusive nature was a bit strange: particularly as Mum was only yards away and her illness prevented her from going into Iris's, these interludes of 'normality' were a welcome respite for the three of us.

****

In June 2012 Mum celebrates her eightieth birthday and we want to mark the occasion with a bit of a party.

I know Mum was oblivious to the occasion, however I think we did it more for our own sake as much as anything. Life at that time seemed to be peppered with difficulties and sadness, a reason to celebrate had to be grasped.

Jess organises with the nursing home for Dolly to be brought to Mum's for the occasion. Iris for once did not take too much persuasion to come and their youngest sister Reese also comes with her husband as did Doris and Rowena.

It is lovely to see the four sisters together; it has been many years since this has happened.

Sadly, by this time, Reese too had been diagnosed with dementia. I know, four sisters all affected by this horrible illness. It doesn't bode well for my generation!

Anyway, there was much laughter that day coupled with the inevitable sadness which Alzheimer's often brings to a family.

It's late one Saturday afternoon around September 2013.

I am with Mum who is having a relatively good day. She has been sitting up in bed, mumbling occasionally and most importantly, has been eating and drinking plenty. The phone rings and I answer to hear Iris, who sounds a bit hesitant as she tells me she needs Doris's phone number.

I have already spoken to Iris a couple of times today but it's not unusual for her to call several times a day to check on Mum and ask how I am coping.

This time however, it's not Mum she asks about. I ask whether there is anything I can do for her.

Iris's next words have me confused and more than a bit worried.

She continues that Isaac, Doris's son who was married to Eleanor's daughter Julie, has brought two men to her house a while ago and then left, telling Iris he would come back for the men later on.

I am fairly sure there are no men at her house. It is not the first time she has come up with some fantastical story. Nevertheless, I had to be sure that there is nobody in her house so I ask who the men are and what they are doing.

"You know, these men who tell you what is happening at the football."

It takes me a moment to take in what she is saying.

"It's alright," she continues, "I know who they are, I listen to them on the radio every week; I just can't remember their names."

Although by this time I am certain there is nobody in her home, I need to be one hundred percent satisfied that she is alone and safe.

"Let me speak to one of the men," I ask.

"Oh I can't do that, they are downstairs in the living room and I am up in the bedroom," is her immediate response.

"Come downstairs and open the door, I'm coming in," I insist.

"No, I don't want them to think I'm trying to get rid of them."

I sigh with exasperation, fairly sure by this time that she is in the middle of one of her 'episodes.'

I tell her I am coming in regardless and end the call. Mum is settled and has started to doze so I feel OK about leaving her alone for the couple of minutes it will take me to go into my auntie's home.

Whilst looking for Mum's front door key, the phone rings again. It is Iris.

"It's OK, they have just gone," she says.

I tell her I am coming in anyway and as I enter her home a minute later she assures me that she is alright and there is no problem.

I look around the house, ensuring the back door is locked and go upstairs to find everything as it should be.

Upon my return to Mum's house I telephone Jane to let her know what has just occurred. She offers to come up but I assure her there is no need; I just want her to know about yet another worrying incident with Iris. We do not let Eleanor know about the incident as she is still recovering from a serious illness and we want to spare her any unnecessary worry.

2013 ends on a fairly calm note; Eleanor is on the road to recovery and Iris is now under the care of the Cherry Tree with a CPN assigned to her. However, 2014 has something in store which none of us could ever have imagined.

29

START OF A NIGHTMARE

Doris has now been employed to care for Mum for around five years and begins to take an interest in her Auntie Iris at long last around the beginning of the year. She pops in occasionally and does the odd bit of shopping for Iris whilst shopping for Mum.

It is mid-February 2014 when Doris contacts Jane asking for both Iris's and her late husband, Henry's dates of birth. A bit puzzled by this request Jane asks why she needs the information.

"There is a duplicate payment going out of Iris's bank and I want to sort it out," Doris says, adding, 'I am going to phone the bank pretending to be Iris and I might need the dates to get through security."

Jane is even more puzzled at her words wondering why Doris did not ask Iris for the information. Nevertheless she gives her the details she wants.

Within a matter of days, Doris approaches me with concerns about the amount of money in Iris's current account. She tells me there has been a lot of withdrawals lately and she wants to know where all this money has gone.

I tell Doris that we are all aware that Iris has been withdrawing more than usual lately, indeed Jane has pointed it out to the CPN and I remind her about the incident a couple of years ago when a substantial amount of cash had been found in the house.

Doris suggests that I should try and get Iris out of her house for a while so that she can search for money.

I manage to concoct a story which brings Iris into Mum's house for a while whilst Doris searches her home.

I know this sounds dreadful and I cannot say how much I regret my part in the deception but I was convinced that Doris would find a fairly large amount of cash in Iris's house and that would be the end of the matter.

However, there is no cash to be found and Doris demands a meeting with Jane and her daughter, Molly, who does most of Iris's shopping.

Jane is furious about Doris's demands and suggests that she speaks to Iris if she wants to know what she does with her money.

Molly too is indignant and outraged at Doris's implication, nevertheless she agrees to meet with Doris at Mum's house on Friday 21 February.

As I am at Mum's at the time I too attend the meeting along with Jane and another of her daughters, Aileen.

Shortly before she arrives at Mum's, I speak to Doris on the phone and she says, "I have been thinking about Iris's spare front door key which is kept at your mum's and am wondering whether someone has been going into Iris's when she is not there."

I can hardly believe my ears. "Are you actually suggesting that somebody in my family has been sneaking into Iris's house and terrorising her, because that is what it sounds like!"

"Well it has crossed my mind."

Her words have me flabbergasted. "My God," I exclaim, "that is even worse than suggesting we have been stealing from her." She made no further comment.

I decide not to tell Jane and Molly about this conversation; I thought her words would only serve to inflame an already contentious situation.

At the meeting Doris produces a piece of paper with some figures on it and suggests that Molly has been stealing from Iris over a sustained period.

Whilst Molly agrees that most of the withdrawals from Iris's account have been made by her, this was at Iris's request, adding, "It is none of my business how much Iris choses to take from her bank, nor for that matter is it any of yours."

If the meeting started off badly, there was only ever going to be one direction it would take; tempers flare and Jane cannot contain her outrage, reminding Doris of the many worrying incidents with Iris over recent years which she and her sister had ignored, and yet here she is showing a great deal of concern about her auntie's finances.

Don't get me wrong, I am not for a moment suggesting that the prospect of somebody stealing from Iris isn't abominable, but I knew that this was not the case.

I know what Iris did with her money, as does all of my family.

I have already mentioned Iris and Henry's generosity towards me and my sisters and this continued to be the case throughout our entire lives and was carried on with each new generation even after Henry had passed away.

Iris insisted on buying Eleanor's son John a new winter coat every year since his MS diagnosis twelve years earlier.

Molly too received a new coat every year after she had suffered a long illness when she was just sixteen.

Molly had spent four weeks in hospital following a diagnosis of Graves' disease – an autoimmune disorder which can lead to an overactive thyroid: Following surgery, Molly was left with a long scar across her throat and Iris insisted that the winter coat should have a high collar to 'keep her neck nice and warm.'

This is just a tiny glimpse of how much she cared about our family and the lengths she would go to in order to help out.

I can remember with such clarity during the last years of Mum's illness when I was spending more time at Mum's house than at my own home. Iris would insist on slipping me a tenner when I was heading home, telling me to get a taxi to the station. Despite my insistence that I was fine and could manage without a taxi, she would comment, "It's my way of helping your mum, there is not much I can do on a practical level so this is my way of helping you three."

Molly suggests to Doris that she should speak to Iris but Doris does not do so. Instead, she goes to the police station the following Monday and makes a complaint that her auntie, who is 'blind and has dementia,' (a statement which will prove to be particularly relevant in the coming months), was being robbed, citing Molly as the culprit.

According to the police report, which Jane later obtains, Doris had told police, "I have no proof of this but am going to the bank to get power of attorney!"

A further puzzling aspect around this time was that Rowena had been visiting Iris fairly regularly over the preceding six weeks or so. She would call in on Iris most Monday afternoons spending an hour or so with her auntie.

In the evening following the meeting, Doris phones to say, "In view of what happened this afternoon, I do not think I can continue working for your mum."

I told her this was probably for the best and ended the call.

If it wasn't awful enough being accused of stealing from a beloved aunt who had been such a special part of your life, things were about to get a whole lot worse for my family.

On Monday 24 February 2014, the CPN who had been attending Iris for some time, was scheduled to visit her. Doris was aware of this and decides that she will attend along with Rowena.

Eleanor and I are also there and before the nurse arrives Doris tells Iris, "Molly cannot do your shopping anymore, I am going to do it instead."

The hostility coming from Doris is palpable; she had been to the police just before this meeting although neither Eleanor nor I were aware of this at the time.

Tuesday morning arrives; I had spent the night with Mum and around 8:45am, I answer the phone to hear Doris who sounds contrite.

"I have been thinking," she said with no preamble. "Maybe I could carry on working for your Mum; I deal with the mail and shopping and I know this is a big help for you."

She is right of course, her contribution to Mum's care is invaluable but the events of the last few days are so unbelievable and hurtful, I really do not know how to respond.

She becomes upset and tearful stating, “I’m sorry, I didn’t know what else to do.”

I too become upset and tell her I will have to speak to my sisters. Just then Mum’s carer arrives so I terminate the call with Doris.

I return home the following day after spending most of the morning with Iris; her confusion over the past few days was acute and when Eleanor and I visit her that morning we find a pillow case containing several toilet rolls, some packs of butter and a few clothes, lying on the kitchen table.

Alongside this makeshift parcel is a framed photograph of her parents, our grandparents, and an envelope which I know contains important documents, or so she had told me on a previous visit when I came across this envelope whilst searching for her keys.

I have no idea what is in the envelope but decide to take it into Mum’s for safekeeping. Talk about déjà vu! I had done this exact thing in Mum’s house years earlier and I am overwhelmed with sadness at the prospect of Iris suffering a similar fate to Mum.

Upon our return from Iris that morning, Eleanor telephones Social Services to ask for help. We think Iris is no longer coping on her own and fear for her safety and wellbeing.

On Friday 28 February 2014, Eleanor calls me with news which is a complete bolt out of the blue.

JANE’S STORY

It’s just a week since the awful allegation made by Doris about my daughter Molly and I didn’t think for a single moment things could get any worse.

I am at Iris's house with Eleanor and we are waiting for a doctor to come and see her.

I came in yesterday with Aileen and when we are ready to leave Iris hands me a bra and says, "Look at that, it's wrecked."

"Do you want me to get you some new ones?" I ask her. I thought the bra had become tangled in the washing machine and it is only when Aileen and I get back into my Mum's house that Aileen tells me the bra had what looked like blood stains and scab-like fragments embedded in it.

I am dismayed and concerned and it takes a while for the implications to sink in.

I immediately phone Iris's GP and following a lengthy conversation with one of the practice doctors with whom I am not familiar, she suggests that, as none of the regular doctors are available today, it might be better if Iris's own GP visits her tomorrow. We agree that a doctor will attend Iris at home the following day.

Eleanor and I are at Iris's awaiting the arrival of the GP, along with Doris who had arrived with some shopping and, decided to await the doctor's visit.

A prescription for antibiotics and cream is left which Doris takes to the local chemist. However, having seen the wound on Iris's right breast, Doris thinks the problem requires more than what has been prescribed.

She calls the surgery with her concerns and is advised to call an ambulance.

Whilst awaiting the arrival of the ambulance, we suggest that Doris should accompany Iris and Eleanor and I will follow in a taxi. Doris is the only sighted one amongst us so this was the most practical option.

I ask Doris to name me as Iris's next of kin as both her GP and the Cherry Tree recognise me as such. She agrees, however it transpires that she nominated herself as next of kin upon Iris's admission.

As we are in a cubicle awaiting a doctor, one of the nurses who had already examined Iris, being aware that Eleanor and I were blind, whispers in my ear, "You should be grateful you cannot see that." She was referring to the mess which Iris's right breast had become.

Some hours later when she has been admitted to a ward, a doctor who was seeing her for the first time, exclaimed, "Crikey!" upon seeing the wound.

I remember thinking, that's probably posh boy speak for 'fuck sake.' It was at that point where I realised things were pretty bad.

I have no recollection of how I got home that night but I know it was very late, around 2:00am.

I am at Mum's the following morning when Doris comes in, demanding Iris's handbag and purse which I duly give her.

Following a myriad of tests, Iris is diagnosed with breast cancer which had metastasised to her liver and bones.

Confirmation soon followed that the cancer was incurable, and going forward Iris will receive palliative care.

A particularly distressing incident occurs just days after Iris being admitted.

Liz and I are at Iris's bedside along with Jess and her son Charlie when we are asked to wait outside for a while whilst Iris was spoken to by a social worker.

It is Wednesday 5 March, just days after being told she is terminally ill and I am under the impression the discussion with the social worker is in relation to her needs should she be discharged.

We sit in the day room outside the ward for around forty minutes, eventually Liz goes back to Iris's bedside to see whether the meeting is over.

Iris is in a chair beside her bed as I approach; she is quiet and I know from her demeanour that she is angry. She is sitting upright, her back is ramrod straight which tells me that something is bothering her.

"It's Liz," I say as I near her bed, "I'm back, Iris."

"I have just been questioned by the authorities." Her tone is laden with outrage. In an attempt to quell her anger I tried to reassure her that the social worker was only trying to make sure she had everything she needed upon her discharge. Her immediate response takes me aback and induces an overwhelming sense of anger.

"No, they asked me about my bank account," is all she says before falling silent.

I too remain quiet for several moments not knowing what to say. I am both livid and saddened at yet another unimaginable turn of events.

Iris broke the silence telling me, "I told them I give money to my family, they are all on low income and I want to help them."

I remain silent and as I try to digest her words, Jane returns with Jess and Charlie.

Upon returning to Mum's house, I decide to challenge Doris about the matter and as Mum has a carer with her and I want to speak to Doris in private, I go into Iris's house along with Jane to make the call to my cousin.

I told Doris about the questioning by Social Services and she replies, "That's because I told them."

By now my outrage is almost out of control and I have to gather myself before exploding. I say quietly, "Well done Doris, she gets told one day she is terminally ill, then gets hit with this crap." I tell Doris she should stay away from Mum's house; she is no longer welcome there, before hanging up.

Within a few seconds the phone rings. It is Doris.

"As you are in Iris's house, why don't you look for all that money which is supposed to be there?"

I tell her there would be no point as she has already searched the house and end the call.

Doris goes on holiday the next day for ten days and during this time I spend many hours at Iris's bedside every day.

Jane, Eleanor and other members of my family visit regularly and occasionally Rowena will visit along with another of our cousins, Sylvia, the daughter of Mum's youngest sister Reese. Sylvia's presence is a surprise as she has had no contact with her auntie for many years.

Towards the end of that week, Jane receives a phone call from a senior social worker who wants to interview her and Molly regarding the allegations. This meeting takes place at Mum's house on Wednesday 12 March and I too am in attendance.

A senior social worker, along with her colleague who had spoken to Iris the week before asks Molly some very specific and direct questions regarding Iris's finances. Molly answers their questions and they leave, telling her, "We may have to speak to you again and if so, next time there will be some difficult questions."

I request a meeting with the doctor who is in charge of Iris's care and at 9:00am on Thursday 13 March, Jane and I are at the nurses' station awaiting his arrival.

Rowena, having heard about the meeting, is already with Iris when we arrive and all three of us are ushered into the relatives' room as, once again, the social worker arrives to speak to Iris about her finances.

After around half an hour in the relatives' room the social worker , who had interviewed Molly the previous day, advises Jane and I, in Rowena's presence that, "It's over, there is nothing to worry about." She says this as she rubs Janes arm then leans across to me and squeezes my hand before leaving.

I do not believe that Rowena, could have interpreted these words and gestures as anything other than that the allegations made by her sister were completely without substance.

The doctor arrives shortly thereafter along with an occupational therapist, (OT) and outlines the severity of the cancer confirming that there is no treatment other than some radiotherapy which might make her a bit more comfortable.

The doctor leaves us with the OT who confirms she is making arrangements for Iris to go home. She advises that a care package will be implemented prior to her discharge and a hospital bed and commode would be supplied for use at home.

I express my concerns about Iris going home reminding the OT that Iris lives alone and my sisters and I will not be able to take an active part in her care.

Rowena on more than one occasion, tells medical staff, "Iris has fourteen nieces and nephews and will be well looked after when she gets home." What she neglected to mention is that two of the fourteen were deceased, pretty abysmal considering one was her youngest brother! Four of the fourteen are blind and eight others had hardly set eyes on Iris for many years.

Why oh why did I not protest more fervently! I thought Iris should have either remained in hospital or else, been transferred into a hospice where her very complex needs could have been properly catered for.

This would have been the ideal opportunity to speak out but I didn't and will always feel as though I let her down in the most awful way.

The OT asks no one in particular whether we think Iris would be agreeable to living downstairs, I said I thought she would and referred to the incident nine years earlier when Iris had hurt her foot.

To my utter disbelief, Rowena says, "and yet Iris says, that never happened."

I couldn't believe my ears but I would soon learn that Rowena was more than willing to spout nonsense and sometimes, downright lies, as and when it suited her.

Doris returns from her holiday on Saturday 15 March and the following evening she calls at Mum's house asking for Iris's house keys which have been in a drawer in Mum's living room since Iris went into hospital.

There are no family members present at the time, instead one of Mum's carers, who was familiar with Doris, is looking after Mum and she allows Doris to come in and take the keys. Doris has told her she will bring the keys back in a little, while however she never did.

A bit concerned, the carer phones Jane to tell her about Doris's visit. Jane is furious and calls me immediately.

I decide to ask Doris why she had taken the keys, pointing out that she already has a front door key so why did she need the back door key as well? She tells me she wanted to put the bin out and needed the back door key for this reason.

"Fair enough," I say and end the call.

To my surprise, Doris calls the following morning saying, "I forgot to tell you last night, another reason I wanted the keys is so that we could paint the cupboard in the kitchen so the commode can be kept in there."

I am a bit baffled at this as I had already accepted her reasoning for taking the keys.

On Friday 21 March, a hospital bed and commode are delivered in preparation for Iris's return. According to the OT, Iris has agreed to downstairs living. Rowena is at the house to oversee the installation. A key safe is installed outside the door and a comprehensive care package is implemented.

Iris is discharged on Monday 24 March.

The tension within the family had escalated during the preceding weeks and the allegation of theft had developed into a ridiculous onslaught of nastiness and unbelievably hurtful innuendo levelled at my family.

Indeed, by 29 March, the initial allegation of theft, or as it subsequently became referred to, 'the missing money,' has escalated to a massive one hundred and sixty three thousand pounds.

How on earth Iris, a widow of almost twenty-five years who was reliant on state benefit, could have amassed such a fortune, is beyond my comprehension.

Eleanor telephones Iris's home in the evening of her discharge but cannot get hold of her. Doris is with Iris and tells Eleanor that she is very tired so she would rather not disturb her at that moment.

Eleanor accepts this and tells Doris she will phone again in the morning.

Shortly before 9:00am the following day, Eleanor phones to speak to her aunt; this time it is Rowena who answers the phone; she is unwilling to let Eleanor speak to Iris and offers no explanation for this.

Eleanor is shocked and distressed at this and immediately telephones me to let me know what has just occurred. I could hardly believe my ears; how on earth could anyone be so nasty as to deny a niece the opportunity of talking to their terminally ill auntie?

Eleanor's distress is clear; for my part, I am downright furious as I try to digest the enormity of Rowena's actions. Eleanor then travels to Iris's house to see how she is.

I immediately phone Iris and, as with Eleanor, the phone is answered by Rowena. When I ask to speak to Iris I am told, "No, she is resting."

A bit puzzled by this response, I ask whether Iris is asleep at which point the phone is put down by Rowena.

Later that afternoon our cousin Dickie telephones Jack telling him where and when Iris's bank account had been opened and how much had been withdrawn over the lifetime of the account.

Dickie's next words had Jack even more puzzled.

"We have been told that she may have had cancer for two years," then added, "none of them picked up on it."

Presumably the 'none of them' to whom he referred, were me and my sisters. Jack cannot help pointing out to Dickie that we are all blind, and, hadn't his own sisters, who are not blind, seen a bit of Iris over recent weeks, so why have they not 'picked up on it?'

Dickie makes no further comment and the call ended. I had intended returning to Liverpool at some point later that week however, conscious of the obvious hostility towards me and my sisters, I decide to visit Iris the following day.

I arrive at my mum's early afternoon on Wednesday 26 March; I go into Iris's house along with Molly. Rowena is there once again and at first appears reluctant to let us in claiming that Iris is resting. My guide dog Jeannie, who has been with me on many previous visits into Iris's house, enters the hallway ahead of me and it is only Jeannie's presence between myself and Rowena which prevents her from closing the door on me.

I brush past her and Molly follows. Iris is sleeping in an armchair and my first thought was, where is the hospital bed? I fully expected the bed to be in the lounge, it had been provided specifically for use downstairs so I was a bit baffled as to why it was not there.

Rowena is watching Jeremy Kyle; the volume is particularly high and after several minutes she turns the sound down.

Iris is barely responsive as Molly sits on the floor beside her and holds her hand, telling Iris, "It's Molly and Liz, we've come to see how you are." It is apparent that Iris is very weak and tired so we do not stay too long.

Within a couple of minutes of returning to my mum's house, the phone rings; I answer to be told by Rowena, "I hope you're happy now, you've upset Iris and if you try to barge in here again, I'll call the police."

I still have difficulty in believing someone could make such an outrageous statement and if I had not heard it for myself, I think I would find it impossible to believe.

I remain at Mum's for the next six days, spending time with Iris daily.

On Thursday 27 March Eleanor is given a spreadsheet by Doris who tells her, "You must get this read to you by somebody you can trust!"

The spreadsheet, which Doris told me had been compiled by her brother Dickie, turns out to be a comprehensive, although not accurate, account of all Iris's current account transactions for the previous nine years.

Doris and her siblings had opened an online account using the bank card which was in the purse Doris had taken from Jane some weeks before.

As well as the details obtained from bank statements, our three cousins had included what they thought Iris had spent on incidentals and food.

The most utterly ridiculous and arrogant inclusion were the words, 'assumed similar income and expenditure between 1989, (the year Henry had passed away) until 2006' (when the bank account to which they had access, was opened.)

Yes, you heard correctly, these people who had largely ignored their auntie throughout their entire adult lives, had spent God knows how many hours trawling through years of her private finances, whilst she was terminally ill in hospital. You couldn't make it up!

30

SO MANY REGRETS

On Thursday 27 March, Iris is to attend a hospital some nineteen miles away for her first session of radiotherapy. I help Doris prepare for the journey which was in a day ambulance and, according to Doris upon their return, had been a horrendous experience. The journey had been uncomfortable and there was a lot of waiting around after the appointment. Doris says she would take her in a taxi next time.

Iris is particularly unwell on Saturday 29 March and Doris calls the GP to see her. As there are several family members at the house, I remain at Mum's and ask to be kept informed about her condition.

To my horror, Cathy, Dickie's wife, arrives at Mum's to ask whether we had any Oramorph; the liquid morphine pain killing medication which Iris had been prescribed whilst in hospital. We often have this with Mum's myriad of medication. I am outraged to learn that this vital medication so essential for Iris's comfort has been allowed to run out.

The day just goes from bad to worse when I am informed later by Charlie that, whilst visiting Iris in her bedroom, he noticed a baby monitor with camera, directed toward her bed.

Iris suffers from paranoia and for many years has lived with her curtains permanently closed because she fears people are watching her. Doris and Rowena are fully aware of this. I consider this latest revelation just one more assault upon my auntie's welfare and dignity.

It is lovely to see Iris sitting in her lounge the following day. She appears really well; and Jane and I spend most of the morning with her.

On Monday 31 March Iris has to attend hospital again for radiotherapy. Doris organises a hackney cab for the journey.

I am with Iris just before she leaves. It takes around half an hour to settle her into a wheelchair before leaving the house. She is confused and distressed as Doris, Dickie and Cathy struggle to put her into the wheelchair.

It will always be a huge source of regret that I stood by and allowed them to do this to my beloved auntie. I wish more than anything I had told them to go to hell and leave her alone. I believe any benefit derived from the radiotherapy was far outweighed by the distress caused during the thirty eight mile round trip. Remember, Iris was blind, she was extremely weak with a horrific wound on her breast and, by choice, had not been out of her street, apart from two family funerals, for almost nine years. Anyone who has travelled any distance in a hackney cab will know that they are not the most comfortable modes of transport, and I can only imagine that sitting in a wheelchair in one would only exacerbate the discomfort.

On Tuesday 1 April I return home after spending a couple of hours that morning with Iris who seems to be in good spirits. She is chatty and laughing and it is lovely to see her in such good form.

On this occasion, my cousin Sylvia is also there although Iris does not realise who Sylvia is, saying to me, "This other woman is looking after me today."

Upon my return home at around 7:00pm I phone my mum's house to be told that my niece Aileen, had phoned Iris and, once again, a member of my family was denied the opportunity to speak to Iris, by Rowena.

I phone Iris on three separate occasions over the next thirty minutes and on each occasion the phone is picked up and then immediately put down without anyone speaking. I cannot say with absolute certainty that it is Rowena who has put the phone down on me but her car was outside the house during this period and it was she who had spoken to Aileen just minutes before my calls.

31

JANE'S DESPAIR

Liz has gone home for a few days; I am with Mum and will be staying here tonight.

It's Wednesday 2 April. I haven't seen Iris today so Paul says he will come and sit with Mum whilst I spend some time with Iris.

As I approach the front door, I am concerned to hear Iris shouting. I cannot make out what she is saying and I gingerly knock at the door which is opened by Doris. Iris is at the top of the stairs and continues shouting. This time I hear her clearly as she shouts, "This is not my bleedin' house!"

I let Iris know that I am here. Iris shouts to Doris, "You keep Jane out of this, leave her alone," then to me, "Jane, don't you get involved in what has been going on in here today."

Just then the phone rings and Doris answers it. Iris is coming down the stairs by this time and she shouts, "I can't even answer my own phone." Doris tries to placate Iris but her words offered no comfort.

I do not know who was on the phone. I take hold of Iris's hands; she has reached the bottom of the stairs by this time. I try to comfort her but my own emotions are overwhelming; I have never seen her in such a state and I am at a loss to know what to do other than try to reassure her that I am there for her. I am saddened more than I can say.

Iris repeats that Doris should not involve me in what has been going on today. I don't know what she means however I do know that Doris, Rowena and Dickie have been in Iris's home for several hours earlier today; all three cars were outside most of the afternoon.

I tell Iris that I am staying at Mum's tonight and she should phone me if she wants me and I will come straight back to her. She replies, "Don't you tell your mother what has been going on in here today, it will make her vomit."

I have no idea what she means but I am really upset to see her in such distress.

I would learn later that, sometime after my visit, Doris had phoned the crisis team at the Cherry Tree to ask whether she could give Iris some extra Oramorph as she was very distressed and cannot be calmed down.

I return to Mum's house and tell Paul what has happened. I just sit crying about what I have just witnessed.

32

HANDWRITTEN LETTER

It's good to be back at home although my thoughts are forever with Iris and my sisters in Liverpool.

On Thursday 3 April I spend the day with some friends who have a holiday home in the beautiful Argyle countryside. I thought the tranquility of my surroundings would offer a brief respite from the endless despair and sadness which has been tearing me apart for the past six weeks.

I have purposely turned off my phone so as not to be given any more distressing news from my family. Selfish, I know, but I so desperately need a break from the turmoil which has inexplicably visited me and my sisters recently.

Shortly after my return home, Jane telephones from Mum's to say she and Aileen have just come from Iris's house where Aileen has found a handwritten letter on the mantelpiece stating, 'If it were felt appropriate that Iris should be taken into a nursing home, we the family would sign the necessary papers for this'. The letter is addressed to 'the multi-discipline team', (MDT) and signed by Rowena in her capacity as a nurse.

Upon finding this letter Aileen goes upstairs where she telephones Eleanor and reads the letter to her.

She does not mention the letter to Jane until they return to Mum's. Doris, who is looking after Iris, is not present at the time, she had left for a brief period as soon as Jane and Aileen arrived.

Upon learning of the letter I have to admit to feeling a sense of relief; my immediate response to Jane was, "that's the first sensible thing they have done for her!"

33

ELEANOR'S MISERY

Has this nightmare really only been going on for six weeks, so much has happened and it seems like forever ago since I felt even halfway happy.

I feel - God what do I feel - I really don't know. I'm tired... no, make that exhausted! I could say I am sad but sad doesn't begin to describe how wretched I feel.

I cannot stop crying, I become breathless with the slightest exertion and I know my blood sugars are all over the place.

The years of care my sisters and I have provided for our mum have taken their toll on all of us and my recent illness only eight months ago has made me less able to participate in Mum's care as fully as I would like but Liz and Jane are insistent that I take things easy for a while.

I spent six days in intensive care last August after suffering kidney failure, following two weeks of feeling unwell with sickness and diarrhoea during which time I had gone to my GP who referred me to A&E, only to be fobbed off twice by the hospital and sent home following perfunctory examination.

I knew I wasn't right but what was I to do! I just hoped every day that I would start to feel better; instead I became more and more unwell. I was eventually admitted as an emergency after collapsing at home owing to kidney failure. I was put on dialysis and would learn much later that my family were told I may require dialysis long-term whilst awaiting a kidney transplant.

After four days in intensive care an attempt was made to remove dialysis to see whether my kidneys could function unsupported however, after a relatively short period my condition deteriorated and I suffered a pulmonary oedema and was immediately put back on dialysis. I vaguely remember there being a number of medical staff around my bed and there seemed to be a bit of a commotion. I think I must have been drifting in and out of consciousness as the only thing I remember with any clarity is thinking, "If I die I will be with my dad."

I spent a further two days in intensive care and was eventually stable enough to come off dialysis and transfer to a renal ward where I spent another two weeks.

I haven't been feeling well over the last few weeks since the awful allegations against my family and with Iris's devastating illness coming right on their heels, I can barely function or think straight.

I can't stop crying and I know Liz and Jane are equally devastated by Iris's illness and we are all dumbfounded by the horrible things our cousins are doing to us. Iris has been a constant in our lives and been like a second mum to us, never more so than over the past two and a half years since Mum became bedridden and Iris became increasingly concerned about the three of us; she constantly worried about how we were coping. "Are you getting enough sleep?" And, "I hope you are eating properly," she constantly chided.

It's Friday 4 April and I am staying at Mum's following the awful events of Wednesday when Julie ranted at me about my emotional state. After some consideration I decide that my husband and children may be right in their fears that I am on the brink of a nervous breakdown and so, on Wednesday afternoon, I took myself to A&E where I had a consultation with a mental health specialist.

I was told that my feelings are not surprising given what is going on in my life at present. Returning home in a taxi, I felt almost relieved that I was diagnosed with stress and anxiety rather than any underlying mental health issues. I could never have imagined that things were about to become a whole lot worse.

Leaving Aileen to look after Mum, I go into see how Iris is today. I am greeted by Doris's sister-in-law, Imogen, who tells me Iris isn't very well and is still in bed. I go upstairs to Iris's bedroom and sit beside her on the bed. Imogen makes us tea and a sandwich and while she is doing this I call Jane as I am really worried about Iris who is leaning against me with her head on my shoulder; she tells me she has been crying and, trying to keep a reign on my own tears, I try to offer her some comfort.

Out of the blue Iris says, "I just want you to be alright."

Again, I attempt to comfort her assuring her that I will be OK even though I do not believe this myself.

I finish my tea and sandwich; I don't remember whether Iris eats anything. Jane arrives and we both sit with our auntie.

Imogen remains downstairs with Molly and Peter, Jane's son, who has arrived with Jane.

After a while the district nurse arrives to attend to Iris's dressing. The nurse is familiar with us and is aware that we are both blind.

"You two stay over there", she tells us in a light-hearted tone, as she spreads her medical paraphernalia in front of us.

I go downstairs and leave Jane with the nurse. At around one o'clock, Rowena arrives. She says to no one in particular, "I cannot be in the same room as you lot."

Turning to Molly, Rowena asks, "Can you look after Iris?"

Annoyed, Molly responds with incredulity, "You want me to look after her after accusing me of stealing all of her money, tormenting her and ignoring her illness for two years?"

Rowena turns to me asking the same question. I find this strange as she was present at the hospital prior to Iris's discharge when it was made clear to medical staff that my sisters and I would not be able to take an active part in Iris's care.

Rowena goes into the kitchen and makes a phone call. I don't know to whom but I hear her say amongst other things, "and our poor Annie is in there on her own."

I can hardly believe what I am hearing; she knows that my mum is never left alone, not to mention the fact that she could not possibly have known who was at Mum's home at that moment. Her blatant lie takes me aback.

I go upstairs to let Jane know what is going on. I am absolutely furious at what Rowena has said and done. Jane goes downstairs and I remain with Iris and the nurse. When Jane reaches the bottom of the stairs I hear Rowena say, "Jane, can you look after Iris as I cannot be in the same room as you," adding "I am recording this."

Jane said "No. Who said you cannot be in the same room as us?"

"I am not prepared to say," she replies.

Just then a lady turns up on the doorstep asking to see Jane.

"That's me," Jane replies.

The stranger introduces herself as Brenda Lamb from the Cherry Tree, someone with whom Jane has spoken about Iris's mental health on numerous occasions although this is the first time they are meeting.

She explains that she has come as a result of the 'distressed' phone call made by Doris to the Cherry Tree on Wednesday evening.

The nurse comes downstairs and said she would have to call her supervisor as there is obvious conflict within the family which is not good for Iris.

Shortly after the senior district nurse, Karen, arrives (again, Jane and I know Karen as she too attends my mum on a regular basis) Jane introduces her to Brenda Lamb who advises Karen that she is concerned about Iris following the phone call made by Doris. Karen appears annoyed, stating, "Doris should have contacted me about Iris's medication. I am in charge of her care."

Karen tells Brenda that in her opinion Iris should never have been discharged from hospital in the first place, adding, "I had secured a place for her in a local nursing home."

Jane and I go into my mum's house with Karen and she asks us whether we would be in agreement if she were to arrange for Iris to go into The Lime Trees this afternoon. Both Jane and I agree with this as we have been concerned about the quality of care Iris has received from our cousins.

Karen leaves for a short while then returns to advise that an ambulance has been organised to take Iris to the nursing home where she will receive professional end of life care.

Jane goes home and I remain at Mum's with Aileen who is looking after Mum tonight. After dinner I go to bed as Aileen is staying downstairs with Mum. Around 10:00pm I am awakened by a loud bang. I get such a fright as I have never heard anything like it, it sounds like somebody is kicking down the front door. Aileen and I reach the door at the same time to be greeted by Doris; she is shouting and swearing, "You gang of witches, you put her in there and she is going to die there on her own!"

I am in a state of shock and can hardly believe what I am hearing as it was only yesterday when Aileen had read a letter to me suggesting that Iris be admitted into nursing care.

Although the letter was signed by Rowena, I cannot believe that Doris was unaware of it as she was at the house the evening it was found. Not to mention the letter referred to 'we the family.'

She continues to hurl abuse for several minutes; by this time another of my nieces arrives having heard the commotion from her home next door. Doris eventually leaves, shouting, as she walks down the path, "You will get your comeuppance, I'll make sure you do."

She eventually leaves in her own car which is parked outside Iris's house. Rowena is sitting in her own vehicle which is also nearby.

I am infuriated as this commotion has occurred just a few feet away from my mum who is in bed herself receiving end of life care.

I call the police to make a formal complaint and let Jane know what has happened; she comes up immediately and shortly after, the police arrive. I explain what has happened this evening and advise them what has gone on over the last six weeks. I am dismayed to be told that there is nothing they can do about the incident as to be considered harassment; there has to be two separate incidents and as this is the first such complaint they are unable to act, however, should any similar incidents occur in the future, I should contact them again.

I would learn a few days later that Doris posted a distorted and nasty posting on Facebook the following morning, regarding Iris's admission to the nursing home in which she referred to my family being 'so wicked.' A bit rich considering she was not present during the events of that day.

34

JANE'S CONCERNS

I phone the nursing home the morning after Iris's admission and am dismayed to hear from a nurse that he had received a call from Doris earlier who had ranted about the care they are providing for Iris.

I go to the nursing home with Eleanor later that day; Iris is fairly well and we sit in the lounge with the other residents. It is Grand National day and in times gone by, we would always have a flutter on this race. We sit around the television listening to the commentary.

Iris always enjoys listening to big sports events on the radio, especially the football on a Saturday afternoon. Her favourite team is Manchester United because, for some reason, she likes Wayne Rooney. I know, go figure!

We sit with Iris for several hours that afternoon and I assure her that we will come and see her every day. She seems settled and unconcerned about her change of environment.

For myself, I feel far more relaxed and comfortable visiting my auntie here; during the short period she was at home, there were one or other of my cousins permanently with her and the atmosphere within the house was strained to say the least.

35

WEDDING PHOTOGRAPH

I speak to Iris on the phone while she is with Eleanor and Jane listening to the Grand National. I tell her I am looking forward to seeing her in a couple of days. The following Tuesday I am at Iris's bedside when Doris appears with Iris's wedding photograph which she puts on the wall saying to no one in particular, "This will make them look at her as a person."

I don't get her meaning and make no comment.

Jess and Charlie are present and, even though we can no longer see the picture, Jess and I begin reminiscing about how lovely Iris's dress was and how handsome Henry had been.

I am a bit baffled as to where Doris had found the photograph as it was not displayed anywhere in Iris's home. It had never featured in her home for the past twenty-three years.

There was a reason for this and if Doris had had any kind of relationship with her auntie, she would have understood this and realised how inappropriate her gesture was.

Upon returning to my mum's house later that day, I am concerned to see Molly, who was looking after Mum, in a very agitated state. Mum has suffered a choking episode and Molly had called an ambulance, such was her fear for Mum's wellbeing.

I attempt to comfort Molly, trying to hide my own distress. Mum has settled by this time but the episode has left her weak and listless. Two paramedics arrive shortly thereafter and examine Mum. To our relief they remain at the house for over an hour, keeping a close eye on her, checking vital signs and monitoring her breathing, before becoming satisfied that the episode has not caused any lasting damage.

I go to bed early that night, weary and bewildered at the events which were unfolding. It seemed like, every day, there is a new crisis to contend with; I feel as though I am in a nightmare which just seems to go on and on.

The following morning, Wednesday 9 April, Eleanor, Jane, my niece Aileen and I arrive by taxi at the nursing home. Upon our arrival Aileen observes our cousin, Sylvia, arriving just ahead of us. She goes inside without acknowledging our presence.

As we walk towards Iris's room, three people pass us without speaking. It is only after they have gone that Aileen tells us, "That was Doris, Sylvia and Dr Tanner," (Iris's GP).

I immediately try to follow my two cousins and the doctor to see what is going on; they are nowhere to be seen so I return to Iris's room. She is very sleepy and not talking.

Within a couple of minutes Doris and Sylvia return. Doris says, "She is going home" and continues that Iris has asked to go home and the GP has agreed that she can. Jane and Aileen both express concern at this development. I just wonder how Iris has come to make such a request when she is barely conscious and uncommunicative.

Shortly after Doris and Sylvia both leave, they spent no time with Iris. Remember, Sylvia had arrived only minutes before and left immediately following her meeting with the doctor.

It is hard to believe this meeting had not been orchestrated although Doris's attempts to take Iris home is more than a bit baffling considering the letter written by her sister.

The four of us remain with Iris for a while; she is still very tired and says very little. We leave for a short while whilst Iris sleeps and during this time Jane phones the social worker who has been responsible for Iris's care following her discharge from hospital. Jane expresses our concerns at this latest development and is told, "Iris will be going nowhere until I have discussed her care with the Multi-Discipline Team (MDT)."

We return to the nursing home and stay with Iris throughout the afternoon. She remains sleepy with only brief episodes of awareness and speaks only briefly with us.

Iris does not go home, the following morning; Jane receives word from the social worker that the MDT has determined that it is in her best interest to remain where she is.

36

BEDSIDE VIGIL

Eleanor is exhausted; we both spent last night at Mum's house and neither of us got much sleep. Yesterday's palaver at the nursing home was both bewildering and upsetting for all of us. I suggest to Eleanor that we should do something different today just to try and take our minds off things for a couple of hours.

Jane and some of her family are visiting Iris and Molly is looking after Mum so we decide to go into town to get her some new nighties.

We complete our shopping with help from store staff. I am with my guide dog and Eleanor is using her white cane and the trip through the busy streets is a bit daunting for us but, with a little help from kindly strangers, we complete our purchases then go for a coffee

Jane phones just as we were finishing our cuppas to say Iris has deteriorated and she suggests we should come straightaway.

Upon our arrival we are greeted by Jane and her daughters along with Jess and Charlie. Iris's niece Pauline also visits for a short while.

Iris is barely conscious and unresponsive. Most of us remain in the corridor outside her room and we take turns sitting with her.

Rowena makes a brief appearance that evening bending over Iris stating, "It's been a privilege looking after you." She immediately leaves after this.

I persuade Eleanor to go back to Mum's house to get some respite. The rest of us remain until around 9:00pm and eventually there is only myself and Jane left. We have decided to spend the night.

We leave Iris around mid-morning the following day. There are various members of my family along with Jess and Charlie who spend time with Iris during the day and I return around 6:00pm to spend the night at her bedside. Molly has been with her from earlier that afternoon and has agreed to remain with Iris until I arrive. Having been put on a syringe driver and a second intravenous medication the previous afternoon, she remains barely conscious and largely uncommunicative with only brief moments of lucidity.

Upon my arrival, I learn from Molly that Eleanor had just been visited at Mum's house by Isaac, her then son-in-law, who tells Eleanor that his mother, Doris, is in bits because she had received a phone call from Jane earlier that afternoon in which Jane had asked her a question which Doris took exception to. The question referred to a personal matter about a close member of her family and had upset Doris and prompted her to put the phone down without a word.

Despite being told that Jane was not at the house, Eleanor's son-in-law nevertheless proceeded to refer to the allegations made by his mother Doris, against my family stating, "You only got away with it because Iris does not want to press charges," adding as he walked away, "you want to watch who you are mixing with, they are scum."

It later transpired that he had recorded this conversation without Eleanor's knowledge. This was confirmed to Eleanor some weeks later by her daughter Julie.

Not content with the verbal assault upon his mother-in-law, who up until that moment was not even aware of the phone call made by Jane to Doris, he compounded his actions by taking advantage of the fact that Eleanor is blind and therefore unaware of him recording the exchange.

His comments re "you only got away with it' etc... can only have come from his mother who, by that time, had been made aware that her allegations had no substance and no theft had occurred. She was advised of this by Social Services and police. She and her two siblings had also received a letter from a solicitor engaged by my family, advising in no uncertain terms that no theft had occurred and they should cease and desist their continued maligning of my family.

More significant perhaps, he and his mother knew better than most the effect all of the nastiness hurled at my family by three of our cousins was having upon Eleanor's health, both emotionally and physically. It was only a few months earlier that Eleanor had been fighting for her life in Intensive Care with kidney failure. This, aligned with the stress and strain of caring for our terminally ill mum for a prolonged period and then the bolt out of the blue when Iris was diagnosed with cancer, along with unpleasant and nasty postings on Facebook by some family members, had a profound effect upon Eleanor's health and was almost her undoing.

I remain at Iris's bedside throughout the night; it is fairly uneventful with Iris sleeping for the most part. A nurse came in on a number of occasions throughout the night to check the two syringes which are administering end of life medication.

I go to my mum's house around 10:00am.

Upon arrival, Eleanor, who has spent the night at Mum's bedside, is in a very distressed state and is clearly exhausted. She sobs that she doesn't know how much more she can take. I think she has had a difficult time with Mum but she tells me Mum is fine; she just feels wretched and cannot stop crying. I am dismayed when she tells me she telephoned the Samaritans a short while ago as she does not know where to turn.

I persuade Eleanor to have something to eat and then go upstairs to rest; at this stage we are extremely concerned about Eleanor's health, her blood sugar is erratic and coming so soon after the kidney failure, the worry about her wellbeing is overwhelming.

Jane arrives soon after.

Around 1:00pm there is a knock at the door. Jane answers. I am walking downstairs when I hear a male voice say, "It's Joseph here." It is Doris and her husband who are on the doorstep.

Joseph becomes animated, shouting and pointing at Jane about the phone call to Doris the previous afternoon, exclaiming loudly, "You have brought me into this now," as he continues waving his finger at Jane.

At this point I intervene, telling them to get lost, adding, "My mum is only yards away from your shouting!"

He responds by inviting Jane to step outside. I shut the door at this point. Doris shouts through the letterbox "That was the lowest of the low Jane!"

They both sit in their car for several minutes before driving off. Immediately following their departure, another of our cousins arrives. Pamela, Sylvia's older sister says she has just been to visit Iris so thought she would come to see my mum as she was in the area. Pamela's visit is a surprise as she has not been at Mum's house for many years, nevertheless, her visit was very much appreciated as for weeks now, I have felt an enormous sense of hostility coming from the wider family, particularly as Sylvia had so obviously allied herself to Doris and her siblings.

Shortly after Pamela's visit Jane phones the police to make a formal complaint about the visit from Doris and Joseph – remember this was the second occasion in eight days whereby Doris had caused a disturbance on my mum's doorstep.

After a little while Jane goes to spend the night with Iris. I am to follow later on that evening.

Around 4:00pm two police officers come in response to Jane's earlier phone call. I briefly explain the situation and give as much information as I can. The officers take details and say they would like to speak to Jane. Whilst the police are at the house Jane telephones and says Iris's condition has deteriorated further and medical staff feel she is in the last hours of her life.

I explain to the police that I have to go to the nursing home and they very kindly give me a lift after confirming they will return the following afternoon to speak to Jane. Eleanor says she will follow as soon as she can get someone to come and stay with Mum. The three of us spend the night at Iris's bedside. Iris passes away peacefully around 9:00 the following morning.

37

THE SADDEST SUNDAY

We are back at Mum's house; the room is cloaked in sadness. Mum lies sleeping and is mercifully oblivious to our despair.

There is little to say; I think all three of us are consumed by grief and exhaustion.

We left the nursing home around an hour after Iris had passed away and we have barely spoken since that time.

As Eleanor, Jane and I sat in the lounge at the nursing home, the nurse approached to let us know she had spoken to Doris who had asked whether she, Doris, should organise the funeral or would we do it ourselves?

I said that Doris should go ahead and make the arrangements as she and her siblings were all sighted, they had their own transport and were better able to do the necessary running around. A decision I would soon come to regret.

As various family members join us at Mum's house Doris phones.

"We have been discussing the funeral," she says, and goes on to outline the venues, a local church for the service then onto the crematorium followed by a nearby pub afterwards.

I advise Doris that we will not attend the wake as Iris would not want one; she deplored alcohol and would not enter any establishment where alcohol was being served. Doris makes no comment in this regard but goes on to say, "We thought we would put her in her dressing gown and slippers." Something I thought was a bit strange, but made no comment.

Fortunately, I have not been closely involved in arranging funerals, apart from my Dad's but I always thought that either a shroud or a favourite outfit, was the norm.

Jane however, expresses her outrage at this latter suggestion.

Things seem so surreal; it is as though events are unfolding in another time and dimension; nothing seems real.

Later that afternoon the two police officers from yesterday return to speak to Jane.

It would have been impossible to imagine a few hours ago, that there would be a glimpse of light amidst the darkness of the day, however, such a moment arrives in the form of the two policemen when they produce the report from two years earlier which confirms the incident had happened exactly as we had described to our cousins.

The two police officers spend a considerable time at the house taking a detailed statement from Jane.

This report had been brought following my chat with the officers the previous afternoon when I filled them in on the recent allegations against my family.

One particularly disturbing aspect was Doris's reluctance to accept that the incident had happened as we had described. She had recently expressed doubt about the existence of cash being found at the house.

The police leave after a while confirming they will follow up Jane's complaint.

I return home the following morning with the intention of travelling back for the funeral.

On Tuesday 15 April I speak to Rowena on the phone. She is at Iris's house awaiting the collection of the hospital bed and commode. She asks whether my family want to travel to the funeral in one of the cars and if so, it would cost one hundred and seventy-five pounds. I tell her we will be making our own arrangements.

She confirms what Doris had told me days earlier about putting Iris in her dressing gown and slippers adding, "After all, that's what she always wore."

If ever one small statement could sum up the relationship, or should I say, lack of relationship, Doris and Rowena had with their aunt, this did it perfectly.

Iris had indeed spent most of her days wearing her nightclothes, for the couple of months prior to her illness and now we know the reason.

She had been so unwell for such a long time and I can only imagine that in the latter weeks of her illness, she was simply too exhausted to dress.

It is during this conversation when Rowena advises me there is to be a meeting at Iris's house the following evening to discuss the funeral service. I say I will not be attending the meeting however my family do want to have some input so either Eleanor or Jane will be there.

I consider it vital that one or other of us should attend this meeting as, in the absence of Iris's three sisters, whom were all incapacitated in various stages of dementia, it is only Eleanor, Jane and myself who can give a meaningful account of Iris's life. Except for Jess, none of our cousins had any sort of relationship with their auntie – this becomes painfully evident during the service.

The following morning, our cousin Jess phones to let me know that she is able to act as Iris's official next of kin as she has Lasting Power of Attorney (LPOA) over her mum, Dolly, who was Iris's eldest sister and therefore her bone-fide next of kin.

Jess confirms that Doris is aware of the situation but did not seem too pleased with the news, insisting that she wished to deal with Iris's affairs and would be seeking authority to do so.

Jess advised Doris that she was perfectly willing to take on this task but suggested that she would require sighted help so perhaps they could do it together.

During my conversation with Jess, a call comes through on my mobile. Upon listening to the voicemail, I am surprised to hear the voice of Doris's husband.

"We have just had the police here with a harassment message," he said adding, "Tell Jane to stay away from Annie's house tonight."

I am a bit baffled at this instruction. I wonder whether he does not know which of Doris's aunties had died, or whether he was suggesting that Jane was to stay away from her own mother's house; either way, I consider his tone aggressive and his words arrogant; the call, according to the display on my phone, has come from Doris's home number.

I immediately call Jane and she listens to the voicemail. She is equally disgusted at the content.

In the event, the venue for the meeting is changed at the last minute without advising me or my sisters, thereby denying us the opportunity of any input to the funeral service.

38

A BLOW FROM WITHIN

For goodness sake, how much more, how much worse can things get. This time it's a blow from within.

It may not have been designed to inflict damage but oh my goodness, it proved to be every bit as awful as anything flung at us thus far.

It's Friday 18 April. I am at home and about to sit down to dinner when Stewart's mobile rings. He looks at the display and tells me it is Eleanor's husband Jack. I am surprised as Jack very rarely phones and as I listen it becomes apparent that he is upset and angry as he explains that Eleanor has been taken to hospital as he has been concerned about her mental health for some time. The source of his anger is Jane, who has arrived at the hospital and, according to Jack, is making matters worse by talking to Eleanor about the problems we have experienced over recent months.

Jack insists he wants Jane away from Eleanor although it has to be said that Jane went to the hospital in response to Eleanor's plea for help.

It transpired that, when Eleanor returned home from Mum's house earlier that afternoon, her daughter Julie and sister-in-law Nancy were waiting outside the house for her and told her, "We are taking you to hospital, Dad doesn't want you in the house until you get yourself sorted out, you are not right and you need help."

Eleanor was dismayed and upset and tried to protest but eventually went along with them against her better judgement. As soon as she arrived at the hospital she telephoned Jane to let her know what had happened and Jane immediately went to be with her.

I telephone Eleanor, she sounds bewildered and distressed. I ask whether it would be better if Jane went home.

"I don't know," she responds, "if you think so."

She eventually tells Jane to go home which Jane does reluctantly.

Eleanor remains at the hospital as do her daughter and sister-in-law. After several hours and following assessment from a member of the mental health team, Eleanor is allowed to leave. She had previously taken herself to that very hospital for help as she was fully aware she was struggling to cope with everything which was going on in her life at the moment and, as is the case tonight, was told she was suffering from stress and anxiety and allowed to leave.

Eleanor gets into Nancy's car and is expecting to be taken home. Her daughter tells her, "You cannot go home, we will take you back to your mum's house."

Eleanor states she does not want to go back to Mum's, there has been so much despair and sadness there over recent weeks and she does not want to introduce any further upset into the house.

By this time they are heading in the direction of Mum's house; Eleanor repeats that she does not want to go there and tells Julie that if she will not take her home she will have to take her to the police station; ten minutes later they arrive at the police station which is just minutes from Mum's house

However, as it is almost midnight, the station is inaccessible. Nancy speaks to someone inside the station using an intercom outside the building, telling the listener, "my sister-in-law has just been discharged from hospital and she cannot go home, can someone help her?"

Presently a police officer comes out, by this time Eleanor is out of the car and the officer approaches her with caution as though she were a danger to him or perhaps herself.

Julie and Nancy leave Eleanor with the police and she asks him to take her to a hotel. They try a couple nearby but there are no rooms to be had.

She eventually agrees to be taken to Mum's house and is driven there by two officers. One officer goes to Mum's to ask whether Eleanor can be left there.

Aileen is there looking after Mum and she is shocked at this development and insists that Eleanor should come in immediately. Eleanor is brought in and collapses into Aileen's arms; it is almost 1:00am by this time and considering the awful experience over the past eight hours since she left there, it is little wonder that she is exhausted and upset.

Aileen makes some tea and toast which Eleanor picks at and then she goes to bed. Aileen remains in the lounge with Mum. She can hear Eleanor's sobs throughout the night.

39

I AM SO SORRY MUM

"No, no way, it's not happening!" I exclaim.

It's Molly on the phone and she is suggesting that we should try to get Mum put into respite care for a little while. I am adamant that I don't want to do this.

I am crying. I have just been speaking to Jane who is equally distressed, there have been some more unpleasant postings on Facebook and Jane tells me that Aileen had a voicemail from someone claiming to be a police officer, who told her she had to come to Brookvale police station straight away. The message did not say what it was about but advised her to ask for a particular police officer. Aileen was naturally concerned and had telephoned the station to be told that there was no such police officer of that name, nor was there any record of anybody from the station contacting her.

There is no way of knowing whether this malicious message is connected to the onslaught of unpleasantness my family have endured over recent weeks, nevertheless it had Jane overwhelmed by everything.

The episode with Eleanor yesterday seems to have been the last straw for all three of us. I think we are all beyond breaking point.

It is Saturday morning, almost a week since Iris passed away and just three days before her funeral. Molly seems to have adopted an air of authority as she tells me, "You need a break, the three of you are falling apart; you can't carry on like this."

I tell Molly I will be at Mum's house tomorrow and will look after Mum so that Jane and Eleanor can have a break.

"No, no," she insists, "you all need a rest and I am going to make the arrangements for Nanny to go into care; it only needs to be for a short while, perhaps a week."

I cannot stop crying. I do not have the emotional energy to protest anymore but I feel so wretched and bereft. I am completely overwhelmed with sadness and once more feel utterly helpless and cloaked in despair.

We end the call and I am still crying, I cannot bear the thought of Mum being put into care but I know Molly is right, all three of us are on our knees. The last few months have been like a horrible nightmare and the death of our auntie last week is still hard to accept, her illness was so sudden and unexpected.

I am sitting on the bed following my conversation with Molly and I simply stare into space with a million thoughts going through my head. I think about everything and nothing. I sit like this for, well I don't know how long: it may have been ten minutes or it could have been an hour.

"Oh what are we going to do, what are we going to do?" I say out loud. It has become a mantra over the years since mums Alzheimer's diagnosis and as usual, the answer to this much asked question is, "I don't know."

I start to feel sick; I have barely eaten in weeks and seem to have a permanent headache these days. I know

I have lost a lot of weight since this horrible episode started and right now it is impossible to think that I will ever be happy again.

It is mid-morning on Monday 21 April. Mum was brought to the nursing home yesterday and I have come to spend some time with her. I am also going to meet the social worker who arranged Mum's placement here. I am so familiar with this place; this is where Iris spent the last ten days of her life and the nurses and care workers got to know me during the time I was visiting.

One of the nurses is in with Mum when I arrive with my guide dog, Jeannie. She assures me that Mum is perfectly comfortable and settled. I tell her I will be in everyday to sit with Mum and she says, "You should cut yourself some slack, your mum is fine and we will look after her, the reason she is here is to help you and your sisters."

The nurse leaves and I spend some time with Mum stroking her forehead and gritting my teeth in an attempt to stem the tears which threaten to spill over. My throat constricts and feels ready to explode. I can contain my sobs no longer and I just hold Mum's hand telling her, "Everything is alright we are all OK and you will be home soon."

I have no idea whether she hears or understands any of this.

The social worker appears and introduces herself as Maggie. We had spoken on the phone this morning but we are meeting here for the first time. I tell her I am Annie's middle daughter and tell her a bit about my mum.

She asks how my sisters and I are. I get the impression that she is more concerned about the three of us than she is about Mum. She tells me she is familiar with the problems over recent weeks and I once again feel the lump in my throat. In an attempt to lighten my sadness I tell her, “Mum was a formidable lady before she was struck down with this awful illness.”

To my surprise Maggie says, “From what I hear the three of you are pretty formidable yourselves.”

I don’t know what to make of this but suppose she is aware of our recent problems.

We chat for a little while then Maggie leaves.

I eventually leave, telling staff that I will come back on Wednesday. I cannot come tomorrow as Iris’s funeral is then. The carer squeezes my hand. I think this is a gesture of sympathy, she was one of Iris’s main carers and I used to chat with her when I visited Iris.

I walk out of the building with the all too familiar lump in my throat and as soon as I get outside, I can contain myself no longer. I wail and tears stream down my cheeks. I am oblivious to my surroundings and don’t care that people may be looking at me.

I mutter through the tears, “Oh Mum, I’m sorry, I am so sorry; I don’t know what to do.”

I walk toward Mum’s home; it is probably around a forty minute walk and on another occasion I would take a taxi but today I can’t bear to face anybody.

It is a pleasant day and I think the walk might help me sort a few things out in my head.

I eventually stop crying and am passing a park where I sometimes take Jeannie for a run. I don’t have to rush, I remind myself, I am only going back to an empty house so I just go to the park. I sense Jeannie’s anticipation as I walk through the park gates; she starts to quicken her step knowing that she is going to have some fun. I take off her harness and lead and she bolts away at speed. I know she won't go far, she always keeps me in her sight even though she is not in mine.

I feel a bit better as I hear Jeannie thundering around the field and when I call upon her she is immediately at my side. She is such a comfort and I know she feels my despair and sadness, coming to sit beside me when I am crying and nuzzling into me when I feel like I simply cannot go on anymore.

After about half an hour in the park I tell Jeannie, "Come on little girl, let's go home." I am feeling quite a bit better and walk the remaining twenty minutes or so to Mum's house.

I put the key in the door and step inside; immediately I am assailed by an overwhelming feeling of emptiness coupled with the unmistakable sense of Mum's presence.

Scents which I had never noticed when Mum lay in the hospital bed in the lounge over the past two and a half years hit me and once more the tears start to flow.

The house is eerily silent: gone is the imperceptible hum from the air flow mattress which I hadn't noticed was there until it fell silent. The medicated hospital-like aroma lingers along with washing powder and cleaning paraphernalia as well as a faint smell of stale urine.

I relieve Jeannie of her harness and take off my jacket. I stand in the middle of the room looking at the empty bed and feel utterly lost.

I take a few deep breaths and try to buck myself up. "Oh well Jeannie, it's just me and you for now, let's go and have a cuppa and then it will be time for your dinner." I try to relax with my tea and a chocolate biscuit and I slowly begin to feel a bit better.

I finish my cuppa and, although I am not cold, wrap myself up in the fleecy blanket which is draped across the couch and I lie down trying to relax. Jeannie lies beside the couch and as usual, her closeness offers me an enormous comfort and helps to assuage the misery I feel right now.

I drift off and awake with a start, immediately jumping to my feet to check on Mum before remembering her bed lies empty. Once again I am hit by the sadness I felt upon entering the house a while ago.

I rally and tell Jeannie, "Come on then, let's get you fed."

Presently, I phone Eleanor who is back at home; her voice is so small and she sounds so miserable that the sense of despair I felt earlier hits me anew and I feel like I am falling into an endless hole of hopelessness.

"Get hold of yourself!" I chastise myself as I attempt to lighten my tone and convey a lightheartedness which I do not feel.

I talk about my visit with Mum, telling Eleanor that she seems to be really settled and no worse for her change of environment. I talk about the social worker whom I met today and tell Eleanor she is lovely and seems to be really concerned about the three of us. Eleanor says very little, just the occasional oh or a mumbled hmmm and her responses only serve to worry me, she has already said she will not be attending Iris's funeral as she can't bear any further distress.

This whole episode has wreaked so much havoc upon my family and Eleanor in particular seems to be spiraling into unreachable depths. I fear that she will never recover and am frightened about what the future holds for her.

40

STRANGERS

Tuesday morning arrives and today my feelings are hard to define; an overwhelming sense of dread seems to eclipse everything. I don't fully understand my feelings, all I know for sure is that I wish the day was over.

The prospect of facing those members of my family whom have been responsible for so much despair and heartache for my sisters and I is so awful that during my restless night, I actually considered not attending the funeral myself.

I try to keep myself busy, taking the floral tributes from Mum and the three of us which were delivered to Mum's house earlier, into Iris's in readiness for the hearse.

Around midday there is a knock at the door. It is a delivery of a wreath which spells out AUNTIE and some loose flowers.

I presume they have been ordered by Doris. The delivery man tells me there is no one at the house where he is supposed to deliver the flowers so can I take them in? Fortunately, a neighbour had noticed the driver's difficulty and had pointed him toward Mum's house.

I thank the driver and the two of us take the flowers into Iris's house and leave them alongside those from my family.

It was only when I return to Mum's and am sitting quietly I begin to feel outraged at just one more example of the disregard and indifference demonstrated by my cousins whom, even on a day like today, could not be bothered putting themselves out for Iris.

Eventually, Jane and Molly arrive. Jess and her son Charlie had arrived earlier; Jess asks whether I am OK, she has been such a source of comfort and support over recent weeks and is baffled and disgusted at the hideous behaviour coming from some of our cousins.

I am so far from being OK that I cannot immediately respond to her inquiry. Eventually I mutter, to myself more than anything, "I'm not even on the same planet as OK right now.

By the time the hearse arrives, there is a small gathering of family members and strangers on Iris's path. Jane, Molly and I remain at Mum's front door awaiting the arrival of the funeral cars.

I walk the few yards toward the hearse and I send a kiss from my fingertips onto the glass beside Iris's coffin as I bid her farewell.

I clearly remember Iris making this gesture toward Ben just a few yards from this very spot, all those years ago.

The gathering are soon ensconced inside the funeral cars. Jane, Molly and I follow in a taxi.

As we stand outside the crematorium, we are joined by Pauline and her family. She tells me she went to see Iris at the funeral parlour on Saturday adding, "She looked lovely."

Iris is carried in by her four nephews: Dickie along with his two brothers and Dan, the son of Auntie Reese.

She may just as well be carried by four strangers, I think as my anger boils over, this time not for what our cousins have done to us, but what they have done to Iris.

None of the four pallbearers have seen their auntie in many years until her recent illness when a couple of them visited her once or twice.

We entered the crematorium to "Time to say Goodbye,' a Sarah Brightman classic and very lovely piece of music with endearing lyrics, but of little significance to Iris. I would have chosen something from 'The Sound of Music', or perhaps 'South Pacific'. Iris used to have the soundtracks for both musicals in her radiogram for many years. Perry Como and Little Eve were also amongst her favourites so there was plenty of choice for some meaningful music, but of course, those responsible for selecting the music were not aware of any of this.

Towards the end of what I can only describe as a 'generic' service, which was performed by a Humanist, a fact which Jane, Jess and myself were not aware of until the service itself, the congregation are asked whether anybody would like to say a few words.

I rise to my feet and Molly accompanies me to the pulpit from where I pay my own personal tribute to my auntie whom had been such an important part of my life.

Molly advised me later that, as I stood struggling to deliver my tribute, not a single one of my cousins looked in my direction.

Upon our return to Mum's house, Jane telephones Eleanor to see how she is doing. To our horror, the phone is answered by a friend who explains that Eleanor is being attended to by a paramedic. She has taken an overdose and will be taken to hospital.

My hands fly to my face in despair and, hardly able to take in this latest horror, I become hysterical, sobbing and shaking uncontrollably.

Molly takes control. She takes the phone from her Mum and is told by Eleanor's friend that she is conscious and talking to the ambulance crew; Jack has been notified and is on his way to the hospital.

The rest of the day is a bit of a blur. I remain at Mum's awaiting news about Eleanor's condition which comes by way of a phone call from Jack around midnight; he tells me that Eleanor has been examined and has suffered no lasting effect from the overdose and has been discharged.

Rather than this being the end of what is undoubtedly the most difficult period of my life, it transpired that there was still more to come – But that's a whole other story.

About the author

Lynn Gordon was born in Liverpool where she lived until the age of twenty four before moving to Scotland where she now lives with her husband of thirty one years. The middle one of three sisters, all of whom were partially sighted when younger and subsequently lost their sight in adulthood.

Having achieved a life-long ambition of performing a sky-dive, in May 1994, she decided to follow another long held ambition of becoming a writer.

Now in her early sixties, tranquil holidays in the beautiful highlands of Scotland are the order of the day although she has travelled extensively and considers herself so fortunate to have experienced the wonder of elephants roaming in their natural habitat in Kenya, becoming 'up close and personal' with a black bear in California, sharing a lagoon with baby sharks in the Maldives and being awe struck at the spectacular pyramids of Giza near Cairo.

After retiring from a twenty year career in the railway industry, she now enjoys more sedentary pursuits whilst focusing upon her writing.

Contact Lynn at

lynngordonauthor@gmail.com

https://www.facebook.com/LynnGordonAuthor/

Lightning Source UK Ltd.
Milton Keynes UK
UKHW011814061118
331869UK00003B/102/P